It's MY Wedding!

It's MY Wedding!

◆

101 Ways To Make Your Wedding About You

Jean Ramsden & Corinne Weldon

iUniverse, Inc.
New York Lincoln Shanghai

It's MY Wedding!
101 Ways To Make Your Wedding About You

iUniverse books may be ordered through booksellers or by contacting:

iUniverse
2021 Pine Lake Road, Suite 100
Lincoln, NE 68512
www.iuniverse.com
1-800-Authors (1-800-288-4677)

ISBN-13: 978-0-595-36032-1 (pbk)
ISBN-13: 978-0-595-80482-5 (ebk)
ISBN-10: 0-595-36032-7 (pbk)
ISBN-10: 0-595-80482-9 (ebk)

Printed in the United States of America

Contents

SPEAK NOW OR FOREVER HOLD YOUR PEACE!

The Bridesmaid:

Everyone knows the phrase, "Always the bridesmaid, never the bride." Well, that's me. I've been honored enough to have been part of seven weddings. The stories in this book made me think that if my day should ever come, I would most certainly elope! My laugh-out-loud favorites are the stories about guests who believe they can dictate your invite list—really, what were they thinking? And, the stories about mother-in-laws are all too good. As this book illustrates, when the bridesmaids hate their dresses and the groomsmen show up still drunk from the bachelor party the night before, it's so easy to get lost in the details and forget that your wedding is the day you and your loved one start your incredible journey together. Jean and Corinne's straight-from-the-hip suggestions remind any bride-to-be what's truly important. With that, I definitely recommend this book to the bride if I'm a bridesmaid for the eighth time!

—Eniko

The Fiancée:

I don't know whether to laugh, cry, or be outright horrified by some of the stories in this book, but it was immensely helpful in putting my own wedding issues into perspective. The book has helped me prepare for a wedding that is undoubtedly about the friends and family that we love, but above all, about my husband and I! Jean and Corinne take us on a unique journey into real-life weddings where everything that can possibly go wrong does—intoxicated mother-in-laws, thoughtless bridesmaids, collapsing wedding cakes. As a bride-to-be who is currently in the planning stages of my wedding, I found the stories to be both enlightening—understanding family dynamics, thinking through priorities—and also plenty instructive—planning for mishaps, damage control, setting the right expectations with guests and service providers, and learning to enjoy myself through everything! Best of all, for all the brides-to-be out there, this book shows that there is nothing wrong with making the wedding about YOU! Ladies, learn from this wisdom-packed book when planning for your wedding, and also laugh and enjoy the crazy stories that only make your potential wedding catastrophes look quite inconsequential.

—Min

The Married Gal:

What a great idea! This insightful book shows true wedding mishaps prior to and during the "Best Day of Your Life." A must read for any bride-to-be. No matter how special you envision your wedding day, take it from someone who has gone through it—unexpected circumstances will happen. This book will help prepare you for the worst. Its stories and advice will also help you realize that others have mishaps, too. Plus, the book informs brides and grooms that half the battle is to be physically and emotionally prepared. And in doing that, your wedding will truly be about you.

—Cheri

Twice A Bride:

I really enjoyed the book! If only it was published before my weddings! It will get a lot of interest from all types of women—brides-to-be, old married folks, bridesmaids, mothers, sisters, friends of the bride and maybe even grooms. Why? Because the idea behind the book is very practical. This book reminds the bride that she is not alone, and that both small and substantial things may happen with all the wedding excitement. Not only do you read some incredible stories, but you also learn how to either put your foot down or go with the flow when these very situations start happening to you—during the planning process and even on the big day.

—Carolyn

IT ALL BEGAN ON THE 110 FREEWAY

Ms. M's Story

On Monday morning, Ms. M arrived at her office with magnificent news. She'd just returned from a surprise romantic weekend in Hawaii, where her long-time boyfriend popped the big question. And, she accepted! This morning, the usually quiet Ms. M gushed with bliss and excitement. She spent the entire day walking on air, starry-eyed as she babbled on and on about her new fiancé and their amazing future together. The world seemed full of hope and happiness!

Mrs. M-G's Story

A year and one wedding later, Ms. M (now Mrs. M-G.) and a newly married friend, Mrs. P, sat down to dinner. The wine flowed, and so did the stories. As you might expect, the conversation turned to their recent weddings. Mrs. M-G recalled a mother-in-law related drama. At the end of the very detailed, emotional story, Mrs. P turned to Mrs. M-G and said dryly, "*Aren't you so glad your wedding is over?*" Sadly, Mrs. M-G couldn't agree more.

Jean and Corinne's Story

During fall of 2000, Corinne and I began carpooling to work. We'd both been engaged for a few months and were knee-deep in wedding planning. Although Corinne and I hardly knew each other, it wasn't long before 99% of our three-hour-a-day commute centered on the intimate details of our upcoming nuptials. From the minute we got into the car, we listened, traded stories, and relied on each other for advice and support. From Corinne's invitee catastrophes to my organizational ordeals, we were both running the same rough race! We both had best friends, siblings and parents to rely on, though most lived across the country or around the world. And up to this point, Corinne and I had done most of the wedding planning alone.

On Valentine's Day 2001, Corinne and I speculated about how many people would get engaged that day. We laughed about how couples (like Mrs. M-G) were on cloud nine for about a week after the engagement, until "The Wedding" takes over their lives—both physically and emotionally. Corinne and I recognized how easy it was to progress to a stage where eloping seems like the best option. We also admitted we had frequently lost sight of why we got engaged in the first place—to make official a lifetime commitment of love with our partners.

Now there was always something to do and even worse, there was always some-one dictating how the wedding should materialize. Jokingly, I turned to Corinne on the way to work one day and said, "*Whose wedding is it anyway? It's MY wedding! MY wedding is about ME!*" Corinne laughed and said, "*You know, it's been great sharing our experiences. We remind each other about what's important—love. I wish other engaged couples could have the same support.*" From that day, "*It's MY wedding!*" became our running joke. We also found ourselves applying the "*It's MY wedding!*" philosophy every time we started to lose sight of what was truly important.

Corinne was married in April 2001 in a large traditional church ceremony in Miami, and two months later, I moved to England and got married in a small, non-traditional civil ceremony. Two very different weddings—with surprisingly similar wedding planning ordeals! But thanks to each other and the "*It's MY wedding!*" philosophy, Corinne and I both had the weddings of our—and no one else's—dreams.

Whenever Corinne and I told girlfriends about our philosophy, they would exclaim, "*You should write a book. God knows I could use it!*" Like us, most people had attended weddings or had been part of a bridal party or two. And like us, it wasn't until their own wedding that they realized exactly how much planning and accompanying emotion was actually involved.

So, Corinne and I started compiling stories. First, from our own weddings and from friends who had gone through the wedding planning process. Then, friends of friends wrote to us. And eventually, friends of friends of friends. It seemed everyone had a wedding story to share and the book took on a life of its own. Two years later, Corinne and I had collected hundreds of stories. We chose the best 101 for this book.

Your Wedding Is About You!

While it doesn't have to be the best day of your life, your wedding day is probably one of the most special and memorable. Your wedding day is not only a rite of passage, but also the first day of a shared existence with the person you love.

It's MY Wedding! does not consist of wedding quizzes, offer planning tips and advice, reveal budgeting secrets or tell you everything you need to know about napkins. This book does not explain proper wedding etiquette, suggest wedding toasts, or explain how to write wedding vows.

It's MY Wedding! offers engaged couples, prospective brides, their friends, family and members of the bridal party, 101 examples of the typical dramas and traumas associated with planning a wedding. Real wedding stories from real women (and a few men!) who have gone through the wedding process from the engagement to the big day. The book outlines what to expect when planning a wedding through humorous, sad, dramatic, serious, and sometimes hard-to-believe first-person testimonials.

You'll read the stories. You'll laugh. You'll cry. And you'll relate to some experiences more than others. The accounts will help you deal with people and anticipate situations. Above all, it will help you to make your wedding about you. Note: Those of you who expect that everything will go perfectly…it won't. Rest assured, you will be disappointed somewhere along the way. Life isn't always perfect. Why should your wedding be any different?

Each story contains an accompanying suggestion or two in line with the "*It's MY Wedding!*" philosophy. Corinne and I are not professional wedding coordinators or wedding etiquette experts. The advice we provide in the book is simply the same frank, non-sugar coated advice we'd offer each other! Our aim is to remind brides and their partners about what is truly important—their love. Corinne and I also aim to help you stay true to how you want to celebrate that love on your wedding day, without letting others dictate what happens. Yes, you may have to be flexible and make compromises along the way. But, by no means should you have to abandon yourself or your values completely! Your wedding day is yours and yours alone. Cherish every moment.

Jean & Corinne

THE ONES WE LOVE
(AND LOVE TO HATE)

It's A Family Affair:
Mother-of-the-Bride

My relationship with my mom suffered tremendously during my engagement period. Weddings were all new to me, and I really didn't have any grand plan. In the beginning, I was excited to share my ideas about the way the day should go. But whenever I threw out an idea, my mother would agree or disagree based on her own wedding experience thirty years prior. "Yes, you should do that. Your father and I did at our wedding!" Or, "You can't do that! When your father and I got married, we decided against it." She simply wanted to replay her wedding—but with me in the starring role! I eventually gave up sharing my wedding plans altogether.

—Libby

How To Make It About You

You hit the nail on the head! Nostalgic Mom is getting your wedding and her wedding a bit mixed up. Be honest about what you're feeling and share those feelings early on. Explain that although you love her old wedding stories, what you really want is a wedding story of your very own. Your goal is a wedding that is unique—uniquely yours. If she wants to help you realize that goal, great! Be firm, but friendly. The last thing you want to do is lose a lifetime relationship with your well-meaning mom over a wedding that lasts for one day!

Our families had not met before our wedding day. At the reception, my step-mother walked straight up to my husband's family and said, "Hi, I'm the wicked stepmother." As I'm sure you can imagine, I fenced questions about that comment all night. The worst part is that my stepmother and I have always gotten along. Or so I thought!

—Caroline

How To Make It About You

People simply get nervous in awkward, high-tension situations, and sometimes silly-somethings slip out. Do everything possible to make sure both sets of parents meet before the wedding, even if it's only the night before for coffee, drinks or a quick dinner. They don't have to immediately love each other, but it sure helps to break the ice!

Imagine my surprise when during the ceremony, I turned to look at my parents in the front pew and noticed my mother wearing a white dress! I saw her about fifteen minutes before I walked down the aisle, so she must have changed in the church restroom from the lilac suit she was wearing that morning. I was so hurt by her behavior! To this day, I still can't believe she did such an insensitive thing.

—Becky

How To Make It About You

Bottom line: NO WHITE at weddings except for your own! There are always a few guests that forget their manners in an attempt to share the spotlight. But, the mother-of-the-bride? Ouch! Before the wedding, ask your mom what she plans to wear at each wedding event. If your mom *does* show up dressed inappropriately, you or a trusted individual should explain the "no white" rule immediately following the ceremony. Then make clear that she'll need to change outfits before the reception begins, even if that means driving back home or to the hotel to find something more suitable.

IT'S A FAMILY AFFAIR: FATHER-OF-THE-BRIDE

The day before and the day of our wedding, my father called me countless times asking for unimportant things. For example, where he should go to shop and eat, and how he should get around to all the wedding events, as he did not want to rent a car. Hmmm…taxi perhaps? The final straw came on the morning of our wedding, when he called me, not to see how I was holding up or to wish me good luck, but simply to find out where he could get a soda. I felt like screaming into the phone, "It's my wedding day! Figure it out for yourself! Or call the hotel concierge—you're staying two floors down from me!"

—Jade

How To Make It About You

If your father always bugs you about unimportant things and you always oblige him, he's not likely to change his behavior just because you're getting married. The father-daughter relationship exists on the wedding day, too. A few firm words will quickly help your father understand that his constant pestering is not only a nuisance, it's simply not a priority on your wedding day. In addition, if you anticipate this behavior, ask a local wedding guest to help assist your father with his small issues during the wedding weekend.

Remember that some fathers don't necessarily recognize how to give support and encouragement the way you want to hear it, especially on your wedding day. Be patient with your dad. It's difficult to lose his little girl. Although his petty requests seem annoying, the calls may simply be an excuse to connect!

One day before our wedding, my father decided that he wanted to rent a cummerbund and bow tie to match my husband's. We ordered these months before and he initially declined our rental offer. He said we had enough to worry about. I know he was trying to be considerate, but when he visited the tuxedo shop on the day before the wedding, his plan backfired. A bad-mannered sales rep informed my father that he would not be able to get the set, as only the bride or groom could place the order. With nothing else to finish up before the wedding (ha!), I had to call the sales rep. The set would be ready by 2 p.m. on our wedding day. Well, that's when I lost it! The sales rep knew very well that our wedding started at 1 p.m! After my anxiety attack, my mother called the shop and asked for the manager. This kind gentleman said the cummerbund and bow tie would be ready for my father that very afternoon. In the end he looked great, but I could have done without the additional stress.

—Corinne

How To Make It About You

You could have avoided this stressful situation by simply telling your father, *"Dad, be realistic. It's the day before the wedding, and you won't get the set."* He'd soon get over it. When you sense these familial mini-crises approaching, stay the heck out of it by making sure someone other than you takes the reins. You have enough of your own bits and pieces to worry about!

I come from a family with three sisters, so my father is used to dealing with boyfriends! During our childhood, he never demonstrated any macho tendencies or "daddy's little girl" attitude. Fortunately, my father also gets along really well with my husband. So, imagine my husband's surprise when my father took him aside at the rehearsal dinner and said, "You know, I may be a small guy compared to you, but if you hurt my daughter I will kill you." I don't know if my father had a few too many, but my husband's face went

white as a ghost. Neither he nor my father said a word for the rest of the night. Luckily, enough time has passed since the wedding day and their relationship is back to normal.

—Alex

How To Make It About You

No matter how old the bride is, her father may still feel like he's losing his "little girl." Remember way back when he was your first love! He changed your diapers, soothed you back to sleep at 3 a.m. and kissed your boo-boos better. So, how he tries to communicate these complex feelings may come off awkward, or even over protective. But don't take it personally. It's a very temporary situation—just try to laugh it off!

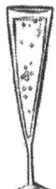

My conventional father wanted a dry reception, yet my husband wanted to have an open bar. I reminded my husband that my father was the one paying for the wedding and so we should abide by his wishes. My husband told me that if I didn't stand up for our way of life now, then it would only be harder when future situations arose. Eventually we worked out a compromise—a cash bar. Of course, neither was entirely pleased. My husband felt that expecting people to pay for drinks was in poor taste, while my father complained about the mere presence of alcohol to anyone in earshot on the wedding day.

—Lisa

How To Make It About You

Alcohol and weddings are often touchy subjects. So are money and weddings! If your father is paying, you are right to consider his wishes. *Consider.* But, you don't have to let him dominate the wedding proceedings or abandon your lifestyle just to please him—after all, it's your day! If he starts to take over, you can always choose to pay for the alcohol, as well as the entire reception, yourselves.

IT'S A FAMILY AFFAIR:
MOTHER-OF-THE-GROOM

Every time my husband and I sat down to discuss wedding details with his parents, my mother-in-law challenged our decisions. We told his parents we wanted a carrot wedding cake, for example, and she remarked, "Oh, Steve would never want carrot cake! You detest carrot cake, don't you, Steve?" This often put my husband in an uncomfortable situation because he was forced to handle both of our strong emotions. I tried to be diplomatic, but our meetings usually ended with us fighting and me in tears the second we stepped out of their house. My mother-in-law was trying to completely undermine our plans. She wanted our wedding one way, and one way only. Hers!

—Heidi

How To Make It About You

Does Mommy still know best? Sounds like your mother-in-law might be trying to figure out the dynamics of your relationship, rather than dictate dessert. In order to avoid adding fuel to her fire, walk away when you feel a "situation" approaching. More importantly, stress to your husband that it is critical for him to support you and, thus, your marriage. In private, your husband should talk with his mother about his need to express himself without her undermining his and your opinions. (i.e. Let them eat carrot cake—if that's what they want!)

The minute we told my husband's parents we were getting married, my mother-in-law suggested, or rather decided, that she would be responsible for the food. When I say "responsible," I don't just mean financially responsible. I mean responsible for choosing the menu and preparing it herself. I wasn't having any of it! She had totally different ideas about the meal, and my husband and I had already agreed to go with our favorite restaurant. So then my

biggest issue was figuring out how to notify my new mother-in-law that we didn't want her help—without offending her. I wasn't sure I could do this without creating friction. My husband and I eventually had to put our foot down on the food issue—among other important issues. Although everything is fine now and the details are long since forgotten, I felt stressed out every time I had to deal with my mother-in-law. I am in no way the evil daughter-in-law, but sometimes she made me feel like I was!

—Natasha

How To Make It About You

It is critical that you and your husband present a united front regarding all wedding-planning decisions. Vacillation leaves way too much room for others to slide in and take over. Especially over-eager mother-in-laws! Thank your mother-in-law for her ideas, and then clearly communicate your wishes. *"This is what WE want"* is a very powerful statement!

My mother-in-law insisted on ordering the wedding favors. She wanted candles, which was fine with me. That is, until they arrived and I saw the tags. Four hundred candles read, "John and Carla," rather than the traditional bride's name first, as agreed. I cried, "oy vey" to myself and let it go. Needless to say, that was the first sign of our future together. "Mommy's Little Boy" always had to be first. I'll leave it at that, as you can likely guess what happened later.

—Carla

How To Make It About You

A mother losing her son is not unlike a father losing his daughter. Both parents may act strangely throughout the planning stages and possibly even on the wedding day, since they are having to "let go" of their "baby" in a very public way. A wedding is also often seen as the last chance for a mother to "do something" for her son, the groom, before the bride "takes over." Having said all of that, recognize that your husband chose you to be his wife, and not to be his mother. These are two very different roles. Refuse to fight over them!

My mother-in-law has been known to get sloshed at parties, and my husband and I knew our wedding would be no different. Planning ahead, my husband asked his mom to go easy on the booze at our wedding. We also prearranged for her sister to drive her home when the party finished. On our wedding day, as expected, my mother-in-law was drunk midway through the reception. She got into a confrontation with her sister who angrily left the reception early. I hadn't yet realized she'd left until the best man and his wife approached me. My new mother-in-law was drooped over the best man's shoulder to keep from falling down! Turns out she wanted a ride home in the limousine with us, since her sister was gone. I was about to say something harsh when the best man saved the day. He insisted on taking her home, as "it was only right for the bride and groom to leave their wedding alone." Thank you! After a few drunken comments back and forth, she relented.

—Brenda

How To Make It About You

Firstly, it will do absolutely no good to try and reason with your drunk-as-a-skunk mother-in-law. And secondly, don't fret about her drunken display. Ultimately, guests will remember her foolish behavior (even if she hasn't a clue), which is by no means a reflection of you and your husband. Good thing the best man stepped up! A trusted trouble-shooting team, including several designated drivers, is always great to keep up your sleeves to deal with wedding-day dilemmas. You never know when they might come in handy!

It's A Family Affair:
Father-of-the-Groom

My husband's parents came to visit to help us pick out the wedding flowers. That same day, my father-in-law's college football team, which was also my husband's, was playing a big game in town. We had all planned on watching the game on TV after the flowers were chosen. But, my husband's father had a different agenda. On the way to the florist he presented two tickets for the game. "Let the girls pick the flowers, son, and you and I can go to the game! Just like old times!" I was caught between a rock and a hard place. Not wanting to appear like a nag, I let him go to the game, and spent an uncomfortable afternoon at the florist with his mother.

—Dani

How To Make It About You

Ten-yard penalty! Intentional roughing of the quarterback! Although your husband's father made the wedding-related outing about what he wanted to do, you shouldn't take it personally. Some fathers don't consider wedding planning a big deal, especially since the bride typically takes care of things. To them, flowers may be an insignificant item. Agree to choose the flowers, and communicate to your husband and father-in-law that you expect not so much as a peep about your final selection. They gave up those rights when they chose to attend the game instead of helping you out. You and you alone will have rights to the victory dance when your flowers score a touchdown on the big day!

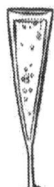

During our ceremony, a cell phone went off as the priest was addressing the congregation. How rude! It was hard not to let it disrupt the flow of the ceremony. Even worse, it turned out that the phone belonged to my husband's father, a highly paid business executive, who was sitting in the front pew. He

not only let the phone ring and ring and ring, but he actually answered it! My father-in-law was sitting there having a business conversation that was way louder than the priest's sermon. He eventually got up, but continued talking to the caller as he walked past all the guests who stared in bewilderment. Then, he stood at the back of the church for several minutes—you guessed it—talking! What could be more important than your own son's wedding?

—Sarah

How To Make It About You

Who do you think looked like an idiot in front of all the guests? Not you! On your day, have someone remind arriving guests to turn off their cell phones and pagers before the ceremony begins. This is common practice in movie theatres—why not at a wedding?

My husband and I encountered a few issues between our families before we got married, but we thought everything had been resolved. We both come from a small town where people tend to get in each other's business. At the reception, we had an open bar and everyone got smashed—some more than others, including my husband's father. Well, he exchanged a few words with my own father to the tune of, "I wasn't good enough for his son," my new husband. The conversation escalated into an argument, then a shoving match, and finally into my husband's father punching my father completely unconscious! In front of everyone! My husband's father stormed out of the reception and drove off. When my own father came to, he was enraged. He found out that my husband's father split, and called the local police, tipping them off that a certain someone was on a certain road driving drunk. He even gave the police the make of the car. My father-in-law was arrested with a

D.W.I. He called my husband and said he would never speak to him again if he didn't leave our wedding reception immediately and bail him out.

—Lindsay

How To Make It About You

Hot damn! What a fiasco! Clearly, it was not right for your father-in-law to get drunk and say what he did. You should attribute this to drunken nonsense. In a perfect world, your father should have been the better man and just walked away. But, parents are human, too! Recognize that your dad tried to stick up for you in the best way he knew how. Before the wedding day, sit down with both sets of parents and request that any unresolved issues be put on hold for 24 hours. That's not too much to ask. If a situation like this does occur, you and your husband should refuse to get involved, leave the reception if necessary, and start your honeymoon early.

It's A Family Affair:
Siblings

My family lives in different cities all over the country, so the cheapest way for us to communicate prior to the wedding was by email. I decided it was important to ask my brothers, my sister, and their spouses to play a part in the wedding, along with six nieces and nephews. As the bride, I sent them emails with the wedding plans, including one that detailed the order of reception line. My brother replied saying, "She needs to chill and just let things happen." The problem was that he intended to send this email to my mom, but sent it to me by accident, since we have the same first name! Sending these emails made me feel more at ease during the planning stages because I knew my family would have the right information, since I was not in town until a few days before the ceremony. Obviously, I was upset at his response.

—Helena

How To Make It About You

As you are well aware, weddings don't happen by themselves. Planning is a critical part of any successful event. Although people may not agree with your methods, it's still important for them to understand what elements are important to you. Be sure to communicate where you're coming from early on. Explain that sharing emails is your way to avoid feeling stressed before the wedding. Let your brother decide if the emails are bothersome. And in that case, leave him off future email lists.

My first big wedding drama occurred when I chose my best friend over my sister as maid-of-honor. My sister thought the title was a birthright, but I didn't feel the same way. My sister isn't a close friend and isn't very task oriented, while my best friend is not only organized, but knows how to make me truly

happy. She even introduced me to my husband! From the moment I made the decision, my sister and I argued constantly. Even worse, my sister acted extremely cold toward my best friend. And when it came time for the wedding events, she made it obvious that she didn't support them wholeheartedly. Despite the friction, my best friend continued to smile. This only proved that I had most definitely made the right choice—I knew exactly who was in my corner, regardless of the title!

—Rachel

How To Make It About You

Although some brides abide by the traditional rule that names the oldest sister as maid-of-honor, you absolutely have the right to choose whomever you want. There will always be tough decisions to make during the wedding planning process. Those who support your decisions, although they may not always agree with them, are your true friends. Those who don't are simply selfish. Explain to your sister that the maid-of-honor title is not just a title, but also an important job with a lot of responsibility. This may help clarify why you chose your friend over her.

My husband and I moved our wedding up by five months because of my father's terminal illness. As I was his only daughter, his last wish was to see me get married. Unfortunately, my father's health got much worse the week before the wedding. On the day, hooked up to an oxygen tank, he was barely able to breathe when he walked me down the aisle. For his sake, we kept the ceremony very brief. After the ceremony, as expected, my father went back to his room with a nurse. He passed away within an hour. My immediate family had been preparing for his death for months and had actually planned for this worst-case scenario. We decided that if anything did happen, out of respect for our special day, my family would keep the news from my husband and I, as well as the other guests, until after our honeymoon.

However, at the start of dinner my brother just couldn't contain himself and spread the news of my father's death to all the guests. Of course, I had no idea why everyone was so serious. At the end of dinner, my mother finally broke down and told me what happened. I was extremely distraught, but tried to hold my head high. But then, the band refused to play anything "too upbeat," not a single person danced, no one wanted to participate in the flower toss, the cake went uncut, and many people left in tears.

—Nina

How To Make It About You

This certainly would be a worst-case scenario. However you try to remedy this, if that is even possible, the circumstances will be heart-breaking. If you choose to continue the reception, try and turn the negative situation into a positive one. Announce to all the guests that your father's last wish was to see you get married. Explain that he also wanted everyone to celebrate life and have fun at the reception, even though he would not be able to attend. Ask the guests to join you in abiding by his wishes. Pull a few party-oriented people to the dance floor while the band plays, "Celebrate." Alternatively, end the reception, go on your honeymoon, if you feel up to it, and have another party to commemorate your marriage after an appropriate grieving period.

My younger sister absolutely adored my husband over the years we dated. They were very close and the three of us spent a lot of time together. But when we got engaged, my sister changed. She became increasingly distant as our wedding day neared. She stopped calling and coming by, claiming we were "probably busy with wedding stuff." I wanted my sister to share in every

detail of our wedding, but was disappointed when she seemed overwhelmingly indifferent, especially when I asked her to be my maid-of-honor!

—Anisa

How To Make It About You

Shifting from "sister," "friend," "daughter" to "married sister," "married friend," "married daughter" may seem like a small detail to you, but not to others! Marital status will most definitely alter the way family, friends and strangers treat you. It's not good or bad, just different. Be frank with your sister and find out why her attitude toward you and your husband changed. Get to the heart of the issues and try to resolve them together. Then remind her that your relationship will always be special and that you will always be best friends, whether you are single or married. You did the best you could by including your sister in the wedding planning. After that, however disappointing, you may have to accept the state of your new relationship.

THE SUPPORTING ROLE GOES TO…?:
BRIDESMAIDS

My husband and I went back and forth about how big we wanted our wedding to be. At our age, and given that it was a second wedding for both of us, extravagance wasn't as important as celebrating with those dear to us. I decided on only two bridesmaids, Susie and Rachel. I selected these ladies because I have known them for a long time, and they have always been supportive. I knew they were total opposites and had not always agreed in the past, but because it was my wedding, I expected them to put their differences aside. Now I realize it's almost always naïve to assume!

Rachel called me five months before our wedding wanting to know if Susie was planning a bridal shower. As with Susie, I informed Rachel that there was absolutely no need to organize a shower because my husband and I had everything we needed. Despite my persistence, Rachel ended up hosting a shower in my honor on her own, and invited Susie. But, she didn't ask her to co-host. That was the first of many clues that the two of them would not work together. And whether intentionally or not, they put me in the middle of their many differences!

—Carrida

How To Make It About You

Power and control issues exist regardless of age and situation, and they always seem much more apparent during the wedding planning! Remind both women why you asked them to be your bridesmaids in the first place—they are your closest friends and strongest supporters. Insist that they be less selfish and more mature, and ultimately, that they put their personal issues aside both during the wedding planning and on the big day. If your friends continue to complicate things, go it alone. You know the drill, right?

I made the mistake of drinking champagne with my bridesmaids before the ceremony. By the time we arrived at the church, one of the bridesmaids was out-of-control drunk. At the reception, she proceeded to throw herself all over the groomsman we paired her up with, while his date, her parents, and the rest of the guests watched in total embarrassment. When she hit the dance floor before dinner, it was like "Flashdance" all over again! And later before the salad was served, my personal waiter informed me that this bridesmaid was passed out in the women's bathroom. Better than passing out in the men's bathroom, I guess! Long story short, we haven't been the best of friends since.

—Kathy

How To Make It About You

What a feeling! What an embarrassing feeling—for this wild bridesmaid. Make sure you have trusted people to rely on when alcohol-related situations occur. If the bridesmaid's behavior bothers you that much, have one of these reliable people take her home to bed so that you can enjoy the party in peace—without any 80's flashdances or flashbacks!

I found beautiful bridesmaids' dresses marked down from $200 to $45. The only problem—the bridesmaids wore a size 6 and 8, and the on-sale dresses were size 8 and 12. I figured that alterations would be required anyway, so I bought them. The bridesmaids, their mothers, and even their friends complained to me non-stop about the "big" dresses. At my wit's end with the situ-

ation—and way too busy with other wedding preparations—I gave the bridesmaids two options. One, they could keep the dress I paid $45 for, and pay around $50 in alterations. Or two, I would take back the dresses, order their correct sizes, and they could pay the original $200 price, in addition to at least $50 in alterations. After all the fuss, guess which dress they chose? The first one, of course—it saved them over $150 dollars!

—Gladys

How To Make It About You

The fact that you actually gave the bridesmaids two dress options and tried to save them money was extremely thoughtful. If complaining about the dresses is more important to the bridesmaids than supporting you, they should give up the bridesmaid title along with the associated responsibility and attend the wedding as regular guests. Simple as that.

If you were looking to take attention away from the bride on her wedding day, what's the most effective thing you could do besides wearing white? Well, how about this…My bridesmaids wore strapless pale green summer dresses. The night before the wedding, one of my principal bridesmaids secretly got a huge tattoo of a snake on her shoulder blade. Her newly tattooed back was on display for all the guests throughout the ceremony, which ensured that the reception talk revolved around her tattoo—and not me. Touché!

—Samantha

How To Make It About You

Sneaky AND snaky, in more ways than one! This is just another example of how people choose weddings to make statements. Rest assured that in the long run, the guests will remember your beautiful marriage and not the bridesmaid's surprise tattoo. If the tattoo really bothers you on the day, have a diplomatic individual track down a sweater for the bridesmaid to wear and pass on a message about why you want her to wear it. That should take some venom out of her bite.

In October, I went with my bridesmaids to select their dresses for our June wedding. The three of them agreed on the dress and found their sizes. When the dresses arrived in February, some didn't quite fit. I guess a few of my bridesmaids had enjoyed the holiday eating frenzy a little too much! Now, I didn't care what size my bridesmaids were, but the fact that two of their dresses did not fit comfortably was of concern to me. I decided not to say anything, in hope that they'd lose the weight. One bridesmaid actually told me the two others planned to go on a diet together.

When my wedding day arrived in June, the two girls had not lost any weight and I think one had actually gained a bit more. While getting ready for the ceremony, the bridesmaids complained endlessly about the tight dresses. For some reason, I felt guilty! Now, whenever I show our wedding pictures, I always need to clarify that the tight bridesmaids' dresses are not my fault, nor are they the fault of the bridal shop.

—Kimberly

How To Make It About You

When the bridesmaids' dresses didn't fit on your wedding day, it was a huge reality check. The two chubby chicas were undoubtedly embarrassed because they gained weight and you were the easiest one to take it out on, even though you weren't the one who helped them pack on the pounds. Just try to keep your cool and ignore them. And, stop feeling guilty about things you can't control!

THE SUPPORTING ROLE GOES TO...?: USHERS

At my sister's wedding, one of the ushers missed his stopover flight when he exited the plane to smoke a cigarette, and was on standby for the next available flight. My sister was not sure when he would arrive though, because it was right smack in the middle of Spring Break, and he had a two-hour drive ahead of him from the airport to the wedding location. And, he didn't have a rental car! The day of the wedding, the usher's mom called the groom to say he had arrived, and was currently trying to hitch a ride to the event. He showed up at the hotel a half-hour before we all left. A very close call! In addition, the usher wasn't able to try on the tuxedo and had to wear it "as is." The usher thought that the whole situation was very funny and bragged about it throughout the wedding. My sister, the bride, on the other hand, did not think it was funny at all!

—Anne

How To Make It About You

When deciding on the bridal party, select responsible people that will support you throughout the entire wedding planning process—and especially on the big day. In this case, someone who would actually weigh higher the importance of smoking a cigarette versus missing a plane over the very busy Spring Break season! Have someone in mind as a back up for every member of the wedding party. People do get sick or miss planes, even on your big day. And if all else fails, go with an uneven wedding party. After all, the wedding must go on. When the usher arrived late on the wedding day, make sure he knows why you are upset, then forget it and have fun!

Our wedding ceremony was absolutely beautiful. Thankfully, both the ceremony and dinner went as smooth as glass. At the start of the reception, my husband and I were practically floating on air. Then came time for our wedding dance. We picked a country song with really special meaning—one that we play every year on our anniversary. My husband and I walked hand-in-hand to the center of the dance floor…and then it happened. A heavy metal song blasted out of the speakers! The worst kind of music ever created! One of the ushers thought it would be funny to switch the song on us at the last minute. The gag got a few laughs from the guests, but I really wasn't amused. My husband asked the usher to put on our chosen song. Finally, the usher gave in and handed the DJ a new CD—and a rap tune blasted the speakers! And then, a teen pop song! After three song pranks, my husband and I had had enough and we sat down, extremely angry with the usher for effectively spoiling our moment—our only dance of the evening.

—Hailey

How To Make It About You

No matter how hard you try to avoid it, a guest or two is bound to make a scene in some way, shape or form. This usher simply chose the wedding to try his hat at being "The Jester" and, as a result, stole attention from the bride and groom. Take control of the situation—get the usher to sit his butt down and demand that the DJ immediately put on the correct song. Then, restart the moment!

I was nervous about one of my husband's ushers causing a scene during our wedding weekend, especially in front of my conservative parents. At a few other weddings that we had all attended together, this guy was typically wasted.

At the rehearsal dinner, everything was set up perfectly, including an open bar that gave guests the option to order sangria or a few types of beers. It was no surprise to me when this usher was very drunk by the end of the night. I discovered that he had downed two beers on the way to the hall. My parents were a little miffed, but kept it to themselves. The following day when I was getting ready for my wedding, I found out that this same usher and one other guy had ordered drinks from the club's bar—which would have been fine if they had actually paid for the drinks. But this was a private club, and it did not accept cash. Therefore, their substantial bar tab was presented to my father. I wouldn't have been so furious, but he never offered to pay my father for the bar tab, nor did he apologize to my family. Thankfully, the usher was relatively tame at our wedding, and some of the guests joked that he was still hung over from the night before. In reality, it was because many of us were watching him like hawks.

—Carrie

How To Make It About You

If it walks like a duck and talks like a duck, then it must be a duck. It is unrealistic to believe that people will change who they are just because you are getting married. So, if a guest has certain habits that you know will interrupt your wedding, then as the bride, you have every right not to include them in the wedding party. When making bridal party selections, sit down with your husband to let him know not only your wishes, but also your rationale. Hopefully, he will understand. If all else, you get to say, *"I told you so"* later on! Quack!

GUESTS & GATE CRASHERS:
THE INVITED

My husband and I were on a major budget because we wanted two weddings, and we had to get the guest list down to a reasonable number. When my ninety-year-old grandmother-in-law discovered that we were inviting only 100 people to our Chinese wedding, she stopped eating. Likewise, my mother refused to narrow her long list of relatives for our Western wedding. My husband and I ended up with a whopping 400 guests between the two weddings—and our budget was shattered!

—Di

How To Make It About You

In the beginning stages of wedding planning, be both clear and assertive about your desires, even though this may upset others. If your families insist on additional guests, and this works with you, ask them to help pay for the receptions. If you do choose to limit the numbers, everyone else will eventually get over whatever it was that distressed them, and you will have the weddings you want—and can afford.

My husband's boss refused to attend our wedding if the guy who introduced us was present, because of a falling out a few years back. We had no idea who (or who not!) to invite. Do you invite his boss, the individual who gives him a paycheck? Or do you invite his friend, the one responsible for bringing us together in the first place? I had my opinions about the dilemma, but since it was my husband's problem, I let him make the decision.

What did he do in the end? My husband probably procrastinated too long, but he did try to get his boss to be more open about inviting the other guy. After his final attempt to convince his boss, he finally spoke with his friend about the situation. Fortunately, his friend understood that my husband really wanted him there, but couldn't say "no" to the boss. Even though he had already booked a hotel and purchased two non-refundable airline tickets, his friend agreed not to attend the wedding. However, his wife was not the least bit thrilled about the whole situation and initially refused to speak with my husband and I for weeks—very harsh treatment as we lived right next door! Over time, she forgave us, and we invited them over for a special wedding dinner for just the four of us, without an overly demanding boss.

—Carrie

How To Make It About You

Invite the friend AND the boss, and refuse to take sides! It is your wedding and only you and your husband are allowed to dictate the guest list. If these two individuals truly value your husband's friendship, they won't force him to choose one person over the other. Can't grown men work out their issues themselves, or at least stand on opposite sides of the room during the wedding reception? Acknowledge that although it's important to think through situations before coming to a conclusion, you shouldn't wait until the last minute to communicate your feelings! The situation and associated emotions will only escalate.

We decided to have a small, intimate wedding with forty guests—about twenty couples total. Taking into account both sets of parents, grandparents and siblings, this left ten couples to ask between our friends and family. A difficult task! Needless to say, we were very selective and deliberate in our invitations. Two weeks before the wedding, dear friends of my husband's family told him they would not be attending our wedding. You see, the couple was upset because their sons and respective girlfriends had not been invited, too. They took the liberty to pass off their invitations to the sons and the two girlfriends! My husband and I were both irritated and upset by their behavior. Especially since we had put so much thought into deciding on the ten couples

with whom we wanted to share our special day. My husband and I were also forced to deal with the tender situation of uninviting their sons and smoothing over the state of affairs with his parents. It was extremely stressful.

—Danita

How To Make It About You

How could dear friends mistake your prized wedding invites for cinema tickets? Terrible, isn't it? In no uncertain terms, it is never another guest's right to decide who comes to your wedding. Be prepared for this type of situation and immediately be upfront about exactly who is invited. If you have to put up a fight, maybe your "dear friends" deserve a "Dear John" letter, rather than your wedding invites!

Before I got engaged, I had heard stories about receiving response cards back indicating a ton of extra attendees. I thought my friends knew proper invitee etiquette, so I would be spared from dealing with this situation. Nope! Some of the friends we invited, say "Bob and Mary Jones," sent the response card back with their names, but also "Lisa, Dick, Bruce, and Jane Jones," their kids names. If we had wanted their kids to attend our wedding as well, we would have invited them in the first place! On several other occasions, the RSVP came back with simply "+ guest." My husband and I resented having to deal with this awful behavior.

—Chelsea

How To Make It About You

Although it might take a bit more work, write the number of guests on the response card before mailing them out. Initially, a few guests might complain, but in the long run it will pass. If the RSVPs come back incorrect, confront the situation head on! Call those who sent the RSVPs back with additional guests.

Explain that they may have been confused about exactly who was invited. Then remind the guest of the people who have been invited and clarify who will be attending. Finally, follow up with a letter confirming the exact number of guests, so there's no room for interpretation.

A number of guests that my husband and I invited to our wedding decided to invite someone else without even asking us. One guest in particular invited a buddy of his to our wedding because his wife could not attend. My husband confronted him about why he decided to return the response card with his friend's name next to it—he said he wanted someone to party with at the wedding! I found it outright amazing that he could be so rude and insensitive, especially since he would know many of the guests. They all grew up in the same neighborhood!

—Jennifer

How To Make It About You

Party on dude, but not at my wedding with some random Joe Schmoe! You might have to remind certain invitees why you selected them over the many others who may have wanted to go—guests who would happily share your first few married hours. Someone you don't even know—who is simply out to party and enjoy the free punch—is out of the question.

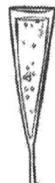

GUESTS & GATE CRASHERS:
THE UNINVITED

My husband and I met while working at a large airline, where we had been employed for more than twelve years. We knew many of the employees, especially since we worked in different departments. Unfortunately, we could not invite each and every one of them to our wedding. Two weeks before the big day, a co-worker approached me to ask, "What was up" with my wedding. Before I could even respond, he asked me if he would be invited! I gently explained that it was difficult to choose our limited number of guests, and that my husband and I would take a look at the guest list and let him know. He followed up three days later and said, "Don't worry about sending me an invitation, just tell me where the wedding is and I'll be there. By the way, where are you registered?" I just gave in. I was so dumbfounded by his ignorance (or was it arrogance?)! On the big day, he was there with his wife and two kids!

—Kathi

How To Make It About You

Definitely arrogance. Don't be afraid to say "no" the first time a friend invites himself. And the second time around, you certainly do not need to be so gentle. A firm "no" should deter future inquires! Self-important and aggressive behavior is simply unacceptable!

Just because you invite an aunt to your wedding, it doesn't mean her children are invited as well. Especially when the invitation is addressed to the aunt only! My cousin is in his 30's and showed up to our formal reception dressed sloppily in a pair of blue jeans and a sweatshirt. In addition to appearing extremely out-of-place, he brought his girlfriend. Excuse me, but can I have

another $50 to cover her plate, please? To make matters worse, they both got completely drunk. Our bridal party was convinced they were part of the staff!

—Dana

How To Make It About You

Rarely will a wedding go by without someone showing up who was not formally invited. As difficult as it may seem, you or another assertive individual should ask the uninvited guests to leave. Alternatively, tell the catering staff not to set additional places during dinner, so the two uninvited guests will not further complicate your already-organized reception. Maybe then they'll get the point. Or, just let them come across as the sloppy dressers and sloppy drunks they are! Rest assured, their behavior will not reflect on you or your husband!

We had a beautiful wedding on the beach, and a steel drum band played all night long. We invited 110 guests, of which 105 attended! Because we were so busy mingling with all our guests, my husband and I danced to only one song the whole night—our song. When the band asked everyone else to join in, I noticed one couple in particular, although I didn't recognize them. When the song was over, the unknown couple split—and so did several of our wedding gifts! Needless to say, we never saw them again. A few weeks later when the wedding pictures came back, one of them featured these unknown guests! Whoever they are!

—Shawna

How To Make It About You

Job description: Must be ruthless, sly, out for fast cash, and cannot be the least concerned about ruining someone's special wedding day. Believe it or not, professional wedding crashers do exist! They aim to take your money, cards, presents and even your free booze. Make sure you assign someone to keep an eye out for strangers throughout the entire event, and have them inform you immediately if they suspect something fishy. That is, besides the ocean.

GET READY, GET SET...

"Dys"Functions: Engagement Party

When we announced our engagement, two different sets of couples offered to host engagement parties. One party was more formal, and the other was a backyard barbecue. My husband and I thought both parties were great ideas, as they provided us with even more time to spend with friends and family before the big day. However, a friend who was invited to both did not agree. She reasoned that couples should have only one engagement party, and she wanted my husband and I to decide which party would be more fun. As if our opinions wouldn't get around, especially to the couple whose party we thought would be second best! Of course, this came from the same person who first asked to see my diamond before offering congratulations when she found out I got engaged. By the way, her response to seeing my ring was, "Well, if that's what you like!"

—Valerie

How To Make It About You

Don't we all have a friend like this? Or maybe we did, and then decided life is too short to bother with someone who is so unhappy that they try and make others feel as bad as them. Having said that, this gal is perfectly entitled to her opinion about engagement party etiquette—just as you are perfectly entitled to have two engagement parties. Absolutely do not let on which party would be more fun, and just plan on seeing her at one of them.

My husband and I planned a special, intimate evening to announce our engagement to his parents. We spent the whole day preparing a delicious meal, sprucing up the apartment and making sure the mood was just right. My husband and I were both excited and nervous when the moment came to

announce our union—we could hardly contain our tears of joy. "Congratulations!" *or* "We're so happy to have you as part of our family!" *would have been a sweet and very comforting response to the biggest decision of our lives. Instead, the first words out of my future father-in-law's mouth were,* "The McKennas must come! And the Taylors! We went to all of their kids' weddings!" *How encouraging and inspiring. Welcome to the family!*

—Tiffany

How To Make It About You

Pass the cream and sugar, and, oh yeah, we're going to spend the rest of our lives together! Parents, family and friends might react strangely to your engagement because they may not have been prepared for such a big news flash. Instead of getting upset, say, *"We're glad you're so happy for us! I'm so excited to be a part of your family. I really love you both."* You will come off as sincere and mature.

For a zillion reasons, my future sister-in-law and I didn't get along from the very beginning. We were cordial at family events, but that was the extent of our relationship. My husband's mother organized our engagement party and, of course, my future sister-in-law was invited. Fine with me—as long as I didn't have to talk to her! So, about an hour into the engagement party, my future sister-in-law threw a drama fit. She started crying hysterically, claiming she had lost her wedding ring. How typical! All the guests spent the whole time trying to find her wedding ring instead of enjoying themselves. Predictably, she just so happened to find the ring toward the end of the night.

—Selina

How To Make It About You

How low can you go? This situation is really about your sister-in-law's low self-esteem—as she is desperately seeking attention. It's also a tricky situation because you can't accuse her of losing the ring on purpose because you'll only end up looking petty and insensitive. What to do? Join in the search party! Your sister-in-law will probably get annoyed because you are acting like an adult versus a petulant party pooper. If you really want to drive the point home behave super, super sweetly and act concerned (even if it kills you!), right in front of all the guests. Then, laugh it off because your sister-in-law is the only one who looks stupid. At least everyone will remember your engagement party for years to come!

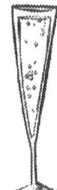

"DYS"FUNCTIONS: BRIDAL SHOWER

Two people who didn't know each other asked if they could host my bridal shower. One lady was a friend of my husband's family and another was a close friend. This wouldn't have been a problem if the ladies were going to invite a different set of guests, but that wasn't the case. Each left it up to me to provide the guest list. Expecting guests to go to two showers was just plain unfair. Therefore, I had to thank the family friend for offering, and go forward with my close friend's shower. When I said, "Thanks, but no thanks," to the former, she continued to insist that we have the shower at her place. When I finally gave in, I had to call my close friend back and tell her why the shower she was planning for me needed to be cancelled. A few weeks later, the friend of my husband's family dropped another bomb. This lady expected the girls in my wedding party to pay for food catered by her favorite restaurant, even though my guests had agreed to bring their own dishes. Completely unfair! Again, I had to decline the lady's offer and call my close friend to arrange for her party, once again. These were not fun calls to make.

—Jillian

How To Make It About You

Beware! Beware of offers to help! Many come with hidden conditions. As the bride, if people aren't prepared to make you happy on your terms, be prepared to change the people or change the terms. You could have avoided handling this sticky situation if you refused to compromise on what you really wanted—a shower thrown by true friends. Go on, please yourself. It's your big day, after all!

I had heard horror stories about hosts charging women to attend bridal showers, but I didn't really believe it until my own party. A neighbor offered to

host, and I thought this was a nice gesture—until I learned the details! My maid-of-honor informed me that the invitations arrived late, only two weeks prior to the shower. Not only that, but each guest was required to pay $50 to attend the shower, in addition to bringing a gift. As you can imagine, I was embarrassed. I would have preferred no bridal shower at all if things were going to be so messy. But it was two weeks before the shower, and the invites had been received, so I went along as planned.

When I arrived at the shower, which was hosted at my neighbor's tennis club, I discovered that she had invited ten of her own friends whom I had never met! These women went on and on about how sweet it was for their friend, the hostess, to pay for the shower, when she was actually making money from it! Her personal guests did not pay to be there, but my guests—my actual friends and family—did.

—Tamara

How To Make It About You

When you found out the hostess was charging guests, you should have called her to explain that you did not need a shower after all. If it was too late to change plans, make a formal speech at the party, thanking the hostess for her efforts and also your friends and family for paying $50 and bringing along all the wonderful gifts. Informally however, spread the word to family and friends that you had no control over the hostess' behavior, and apologize for any inconveniences or hard feelings.

I had two bridal showers—one hosted by friends, and the other in my home-town, hosted by my mother. My mother-in-law was invited to both, but I knew she would not be able to attend the shower hosted by my friends since she lived halfway across the country. Still, I anticipated that she would attend the shower hosted by my mom, since she lived in the same town. So, I was sur-

prised when she didn't attend either! This bothered me because I knew she had nothing else going on that day. In fact, when my husband called, she was home just watching television.

—Melissa

How To Make It About You

I guess that rerun of "Fantasy Island" was not to be missed! Hands down, this is an extremely disappointing situation. Perhaps your mother-in-law was upset because she wasn't asked to host the bridal shower at her home. Or maybe this was her way of avoiding the reality that her son would soon be in the hands of another woman. Whatever the reason, this is definitely not the time for you to take things personally. Explain to your mother-in-law why you were disappointed, and leave it at that. Unfortunately, you can never force others to want what you want. That kind of fantasy only happens on TV.

"Dys"Functions:
Bachelor & Bachelorette Party

My four bridesmaids organized a bachelorette party for fifteen friends and myself. We started out at one of their houses, enjoyed a couple bottles of wine, listened to some old music and reminisced about our school days. Exactly what I was hoping for! At about ten, the doorbell rang and when I answered it, a cop told me one of the neighbors had complained about the noise level. We agreed to keep it down. As the cop turned to leave, he pulled out a pair of handcuffs and then put them on me! At that moment, my worst fear was realized—my bridesmaids hired a stripper! And this was only the beginning of my bachelorette-party-gone-bad. After the stripper left, the girls revealed a whole list of planned activities for the bars. Shots, singing songs with strangers, getting my underwear signed by random men—all of it was unlike anything I would ever, ever do. I wanted to tell my bridesmaids that I was uncomfortable and that I wasn't having fun, but I didn't want to disrespect the amount of time they put into planning the evening. Plus, it seemed like everyone else was having a blast! I just couldn't wait to get home, take a shower and call my future husband.

—Laurie

How To Make It About You

Sounds like you would have preferred jail! What some people think is fun may be outright insulting to others. Obviously, this bachelorette party was not about you at all. You certainly don't want to lose friendships over something this inconsequential, but do communicate what you want (or don't want) way ahead of time. In the moment, as soon as you feel uncomfortable with what's happening, put a stop to it. Something like, *"I don't know what you girls have planned for the night, but I want to spend my bachelorette party hanging out with my friends, not strangers. I'm sorry if you put a lot of work into the planning."* If they persist with their agenda, you can always skedaddle.

My bridesmaids decided to have a weekend bachelorette party for me in The City. I asked if they could also invite my future sister-in-law, even though she was not in the actual wedding party. My bridesmaids had the entire weekend planned, but when we all met at the airport that Saturday morning, my sister-in-law began dictating how the weekend should go. It was bad enough that she had ruined the surprise plans my bridesmaids had thought of, but then she started changing all of them! Naturally, this irritated the bridesmaids. I felt horrible knowing that I'd invited her, so I pulled my future sister-in-law aside and asked her to just go with the flow for the remainder of the weekend. When we went out to dinner, she proceeded to order the most expensive meal, and spent half the time talking to a guy at the bar. Then, she also ordered a bottle of wine and two martinis with the guy, which she put on our bill. When the final bill came, she just passed it to me and said, "You'll cover me, right?" I felt like I had no choice but to pay for her share—at my own bachelorette party!

The final straw occurred when we arrived at a club. We had been there all of five minutes before my future sister-in-law decided the place was lame. As you can imagine, one or two of my bridesmaids were ready to tell her off. Again, I pulled her aside and asked her to give the place a chance. She then demanded that we leave, so I told her, "Fine. It's obvious that you are out to party on your own. So, why don't you have the limo take you where you want to go, and we'll just meet you at the hotel later?" Happy to oblige, my future sister-in-law took off in the limo, which dropped her at another club. We didn't see her again until we met at the airport the next night, boarding our flight home.

—Amy

How To Make It About You

You were trying to do something nice, and it backfired. In addition, you gave your future sister-in-law a few chances to alter her rude behavior, and she didn't. Refuse to pay for your future sister-in-law's drinks and food—surely she must have brought money! Also, call your husband and his parents from the restaurant to let them know exactly what is going on. Ask them for help with the awkward situation, which will make your sister-in-law accountable for her behavior when she returns home—and save you from looking like a complainer.

We've all heard about those not-so-tame bachelor parties. When my husband decided to throw his bachelor party at our brand new house, I agreed, but only under one condition—NO STRIPPERS! Not because I had a problem with the guys getting turned on by the stripper—that I can't control. Instead, I had an issue because our new home was sacred and should be treated that way. More than 30 guys were at the party, and afterwards, the house was trashed with beer cans, the carpet was stained with spills and gum—and one of the guys hired a stripper, even though my husband told them not to. Even worse, the stripper used our guestroom to rest up between shows, leaving ash burns on our new ivory comforter!

—Sophie

How To Make It About You

Ah, good old peer pressure. Refusing to have your husband's bachelor party at your house right from the beginning would have been ideal, and it might've saved him from having to look "soft" in front of his mates. If it ends up happening, confront the guy who booked the stripper, if your husband hasn't already done so, and make sure the guy isn't planning anything similar for your wedding day.

You are doing yourself a favor in the long run because the guy has already proven he cannot be trusted.

"Dys"Functions: Rehearsal Dinner

I had difficulty deciding between bridesmaids, so I chose ten girls for my side of the bridal party. I was closer to some more than others, of course! About an hour into our rehearsal dinner, the guests started to complain about the slow service. My husband and I could see that half the room hadn't yet been served and that the other half of the room was already done eating. We didn't understand because we had made extra sure the place had enough wait staff to enable everyone to eat at the same pace. Despite the tension, my husband and I tried to enjoy ourselves and ignore comments like "If I don't get some food inside of me, I'm going to pass out!", "You're grandmother really needs to eat!" or "Man, this place has bad service." When we finally tracked down the headwaiter, he looked like a mess! He was red-faced, sweating and upset. He explained that he'd lost two waiters. How do you lose two waiters?

It all made sense when we discovered that two of my bridesmaids were missing as well. One of the guests finally confessed that she'd overheard the two bridesmaids flirting with the missing waiters. Turns out that they'd all left about a half-hour into the dinner. We just hadn't noticed. We got through the dinner, but my husband and I were peeved at the two bridesmaids.

—Jamie

How To Make It About You

Talk about losing two waiters, you should lose two bridesmaids! What on earth do these lust-filled ladies have up their sleeves for the wedding day? One can only imagine. You need support on your wedding day, and if the two bridesmaids are not willing to support you, you have eight others who will. The two bridesmaids can attend as guests—without the waiters as dates, of course.

Our rehearsal dinner was held at a private golf club in a members-only room. Midway through the dinner, I went to the powder room and spotted this elderly man looking at our wedding picture, which I had placed near the door. I wanted to make sure our close family and wedding party would have a chance to sign it before the wedding day mayhem started. The man looked me over and said, "You are a beautiful couple." I said, "Thank you," and went on my way. Later, after the honeymoon, my husband and I unpacked our wedding photo. Right smack in the middle was a great big messy message that said, "TO A BEAUTIFUL COUPLE," but with no name acknowledging who wrote it. I suddenly remembered the old man! Yep, a stranger signed our wedding picture, and we have no idea who he was! I should have known better because someone told me that at their wedding, one guest carried on forever when they signed the picture, leaving absolutely no room for anyone else!

—Corinne

How To Make It About You

Let's face it, the situation could have been much, much worse—the old geezer could have written something terrible! Always make sure that you assign someone to monitor the guest book, pictures and other materials to be signed. You never know what guests will say, how much they'll write or, in this case, who will sign.

My husband and I were engaged for two years, yet our parents had never met, since our families lived across the country from each other. The first time our families were expected to meet was at the rehearsal dinner the night before the wedding. An already uncomfortable situation was worsened when, after a couple drinks, my dad began making snide comments about all the expensive things he was paying for, and how much the flights and hotel cost him. I tried to change the subject, but within five minutes Dad was back on his favorite topic. I pulled him aside and let him know that he was ruining the evening.

Thankfully, he didn't say a word for the rest of the night—and that suited me just fine!

—Lisa

How To Make It About You

Sometimes silence truly is golden. But if someone does make inappropriate remarks, don't let it get to you. Years from now, the details won't mean anything. Don't condone your dad's behavior, but acknowledge that the specifics of how much things cost are built into most men's hardware, as well as the challenge of expressing feelings. Your dad probably just wanted to tell everyone exactly what he was providing for his daughter, in his own unique way!

THE LITTLE (BIG) THINGS: INVITATIONS

When we ordered the invitations, both my husband and I checked and rechecked every detail several times before printing. When the invitations came back, we were excited to show them to our parents. My husband's father informed us that we had spelled his current wife's first name wrong, and ordered (not asked!) us to redo them. By this time, however, it was three months before the wedding and the invitations really needed to be sent out. My husband and I called his father's current wife to apologize and explained that there was no way we could redo the invitations this late in the game. She was really great and understood the situation completely. Problem solved. We sent out the invitations on time, as is. As the wedding day rolled around, my husband's father still seemed upset about the misspelling. To make a point about our mistake, he actually spelled out his current wife's name when he introduced her to our guests!

—Doriann

How To Make It About You

Mistakes happen and your wedding plans are not exempt! You can only do the best you can—for everything else, you can apologize, if you feel it's appropriate. Before the wedding, apologize once again to the second wife and your husband's father, both in person and in a written note. And on your wedding day, if your husband's father continues spelling out his second wife's name to guests, your husband should pull him aside and make it clear that no one even remembers the invitations! Let him know that he is not only embarrassing himself, but his wife as well. Then demand he S-T-O-P!

As the bride, I provided an invite list to the host of my bridal shower. I thought nothing of this request, as I knew it was common to be asked. It took a bit of investigation, because along with the name and address, she wanted each guest's email address. The host then asked me if I could buy and print labels for the invite envelopes. Yes, this bizarre request took some time, but I figured the host had a lot to plan for a successful bridal shower. One week later, the host called to explain that she had lost the labels, and hoped I could print out another set. As if I wasn't busy with other wedding stuff? However, again I reasoned that she was hosting my shower. A few days before the shower another friend called to compliment me on the beautiful invitations and the handwritten envelopes. Handwriting? I later found out from an invitee that after all my hard work, the host changed her mind and hired a stenographer whom she thought would do a more professional job than my two rounds of labels.

—Kerry

How To Make It About You

Even if others host an event in your honor, it often turns into an "about them" situation—the hostess feeling as though the title gives her not only all the glory, but also the right to act however she wants, regardless of how it affects you. Let the hostess know if you don't have time to provide something she's asked from you. Refuse to hold a grudge, and just enjoy the party. In the grand scheme of things, the invitations don't matter anyway.

My mother insisted on ordering our wedding invitations. I told her that was fine, as long as I could go with her to select them. Seven months before they were to be sent out, I asked my mother when we were going to decide on invitations, and she told me the job was already complete. She even had the final invitations to show me! Our invitations had a beach theme, which would have been fine, but we were getting married in November—when snow piles

would be six feet high! In addition, the ceremony time was listed incorrectly as 1 p.m. instead of noon. So, my husband and I had the invitations redone. As a result, my mother was upset with me for weeks because she thought I deliberately had the stationary shop print the wrong time, just so I could get new invitations! Was she serious? Oh, yes!

—Mary

How To Make It About You

The audacity of your mother's accusations! The second time around, get the invitations you really want. Also, ask your mother two things. One, why she didn't wait for you to order them. Two, why on earth would she accuse you of manipulating the invitation situation? Your mother's answers will likely be the source of other wedding related problems to come!

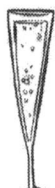

As a graphic designer, our wedding invitations were a huge priority. I spent months designing the ideal invitation, and only needed a printer to complete the job. I decided to use a printer that I had worked with professionally, figuring that he would give my invitations special attention. We agreed that the job would be done approximately five months before our wedding day. When the invitations came back, the heart I designed on the front was off-centered. I called and let the printer know that it would need to be redone. He called me uptight and argued that the heart wasn't "that" off. Maybe not, but as a graphic designer, I couldn't accept anything less than perfect. He was a real jerk—nothing like I remembered him—and informed me that my job would be put in the back of the queue. This meant the invitations would take another two months to complete. Not a possibility!

I had to scramble to find another printer that would put a rush on the job, and paid much more than we planned for. After the wedding, when I was telling this stressful story to my former boss, she started to cringe. What I didn't know was that my old company had actually canned this printer for terrible service. So, my "in" with the printer was actually an "out!"

—Narissa

How To Make It About You

What happened to the old business principle *"the client is always right"*? It seems this is a forgotten practice even when planning a wedding. No matter what happens, if you feel the service is not what you expected, speak up. Learn from this wedding drama and apply it to the rest of your wedding planning, if it's not too late!

THE LITTLE (BIG) THINGS: THE DRESS

My best friend is also a clothing designer and seamstress. When my husband and I announced our engagement she beamed, "Let me make your dress as a wedding present!" We were on a tight budget, so I agreed. Two months before the wedding, my best friend was hired on an assignment in New York. I admitted to my husband that I was worried she wouldn't be able to complete my dress in time. Indeed, despite my badgering, she waited until a month before the wedding to fly home. When we got together, I took one look at the dress and burst into tears. Not only was my wedding dress incomplete, it was too tight, too short and the beading was nasty. My friend got angry and defensive, but ultimately wanted to make it right. She flew back to New York the next day with my dress, promising to have it done the following weekend. But she didn't make it home because she got tied up at work. Panicking, my mom and I found another dress off the rack. When my friend flew back a few days before the wedding the dress was complete, yet it still looked horrible. When I confessed that I'd found a new dress, she went crazy and didn't even come to our wedding.

—Angela

How To Make It About You

This story brings to mind the old saying *"there's no such thing as free lunch!"* Although it initially seemed like a kind gesture and a budget bonus, you ultimately spent a lot of wasted time and emotion dealing with your best friend's selfish behavior. You were counting on her in a big way, and she let you down. Not only that, she continued to string you along, make empty promises, and produce a dress that was neither nice nor memorable. Unfortunately, your best friend prioritized other things over you, like work. Which would be fine, except that she shouldn't have made empty promises or pretended you were her main concern. In addition, after she messed up, your friend refused to attend the wedding. Go ahead and have fun on your wedding day without her. After the wedding day, you may want to spend some time evaluating your friendship.

I come from a family where custom dictates that the father chooses his daughter's wedding dress. I was aware of this tradition through my cousin's own experience, although I hoped my dad would act differently. When I got engaged, my dad immediately set a day aside for him and I to find my wedding dress. I did not want to upset my dad, so I went along with his plan. When we got to the shop, one of the sales reps led me to a dressing room and asked me to have a seat. A few minutes later my dad came back with three wedding dresses for me to try on—and they were all hideous. I had to present myself not only to my dad, but also to all the store clerks and clientele. The dress he selected from the three was big and puffy. I looked like a huge cotton ball! I let my dad know the dress was not my style, and that I wanted to look at other dresses on my own. He raised his voice and said, "NO! This is the dress for you. We are taking it and that's final." *I had no choice but to go along with his wishes.*

After we got home, I showed the horrible dress to my mother while my dad was away. My mother explained that the family tradition is supposed to be something special between a father and daughter, which is why she did not go to the bridal shop, and why I had to wear the chosen dress. When I tried it on she said, "However, I don't think tradition forbids us from adjusting the chosen dress." *Fortunately, my mom can sew, so between the two of us we made the dress more presentable and less puffy. We never told my dad. As you can imagine, he was astonished when I arrived at the church on my wedding day, ready for him to walk me down the aisle. My dad demanded to know what happened to the dress and I told him that we altered a few things to make it look beautiful. Luckily, the music started and we began the walk.*

—Carmen

How To Make It About You

You followed tradition to please your father. And unfortunately, you had to bear the consequences of that decision, with an ugly dress that was far from the dress of your wedding dreams. You say that you *"had no choice"* but to go along with your father's wishes. However, you always have a choice in every situation. In this case, you could throw tradition out the window and pay for your own wedding and wedding dress. Of course, in paying for your own, you may not be able to afford a certain reception hall or so many flowers. You may also upset family and friends along the way. But, at least you will be calling the shots!

A few weeks before our wedding, I was still without a dress. I had searched all over for something perfect, but every single dress seemed too frilly, too plain, too short, or too tall on the neck. Time was slipping away. One day after work, I was running a few errands and happened to pass by a charity shop, which I'd never noticed before. On a whim, I ran into the shop and quickly asked the salesperson if she had any wedding dresses. She told me to check the dresses rack. And there it was—one white wedding dress among all the other cast-offs from decades gone by. As soon as I pulled it out, I knew it was my dress—never in a million years would I have thought that I would get married in a second hand dress, but it was beautiful. More importantly, I felt beautiful in it. Because the shop accepted only cash, I left a deposit. I promised to come back the next day with the balance.

It was actually four days before I made it back to the shop because I had to work late two nights, and then had dinner plans I couldn't break. When I finally got there, my dress was gone. I was told that the volunteer who sold the dress hadn't known I'd paid a deposit to hold it. Another customer saw it near the register, and snapped it up for her daughter. Of course, I was devastated! The chirpy volunteer tried to comfort me with a few sensitive words, as she refunded my deposit. "At least the proceeds from the dress went to a good cause!" *she rationalized.*

—Alicia

How To Make It About You

The moral of this wedding story is never, ever wait until this close before your wedding day to find a dress. If the dress is such a priority, you need to make it one. Take time off work to pay for it. Be late to dinner—your dining partner will understand! Also, let the volunteer know that her comment was inappropriate and insensitive. Then acknowledge that the dress is gone, move on and find a new one—fast! Things happen for a reason and the new one may be even more beautiful!

My wedding dress experience was pretty mellow. Not at all like the horror stories I'd heard from former "fiancefied" friends. I found my beautiful wedding dress in a half an hour upon entering the first bridal shop on my list. When I came back for my post-alteration fitting at the shop, the dress hung perfectly. I tried on the dress for the final fitting about two weeks before the wedding, and while in the dressing room, I heard sobbing from the room next door. After a few minutes I asked, "Is everything okay in there?" to which the sobbing girl replied, "No! My dress doesn't fit." I called back, "Don't worry. The seamstress will fix it." She said, "There's nothing they can do. There's no material left!" She continued, "I told them I needed something a little larger! I can't go out there. I can't face them." I wondered, was she referring to the seamstress?

When I went out, the previously empty fitting room was filled with a large posse of women aged nine to ninety, whose expressive non-English conversation sounded to me like one giant argument. By choice, I set out on my wedding dress experience alone—at least until these women started gesturing and smiling at me as I stood in front of the mirrors. Then the sobbing bride appeared tentatively from the dressing room. The group of women practically threw her in front of the mirrors next to me. And when they noticed that the back of her dress didn't fit by a long shot, they started yelling at her and pinching her stomach. A few of them actually tried pulling the two back halves together to zip it up. The girl began sobbing again and said to her mom, "I told you I didn't like this dress and that it didn't fit me when I first tried it on. Now look what I'm stuck with only one week before the wedding!" As for me, I rushed to leave the sobbing girl and her posse, with my lovely dress in hand.

—Jean

How To Make It About You

Poor thing. The sobbing girl should have never agreed to wear that small dress in the first place! As it was only a week before her wedding, she had to admit to herself and her posse that the dress just would not fit. She should buy a new dress that not only fits, but also makes her feel comfortable and beautiful. The new dress may not be exactly what she envisioned wearing, but at least she won't have as terrible a drama on her wedding day. You are the one who truly knows what is best for you!

Our wedding was two months away, and I had not yet purchased "THE" dress. I soon found the perfect one. However, it was a little on the loose side, and my style is slightly more fitted. So, I went to a tailor who came highly recommended. He said he could take in the dress at the waist and agreed to have it finished ten days before the wedding. However, when I tried on the tailored dress, the seams of the dress and the slip were off. It looked terrible, and I told the tailor I would not wear the dress. He told me not to worry, he would simply stitch the seams together. I can't even sew a hem, but I do have a good sense of physics and common sense. If you sew two things together that natu-

rally fall separately, then somewhere else in the garment is bound to be skewed. The tailor told me to come back in three days. Re-tailored, the dress still looked less than ideal, just as I'd expected. I was so upset. He did not apologize or offer to pay for ruining the dress. He did offer, however, to not charge me for the additional tailoring! Thanks a lot!

—Peggy

How To Make It About You

Use that common sense of yours and absolutely do not pay for ANY of the dress alterations. And then use that mouth of yours and spread the word about the tailor's terrible service. Enjoy the wedding day and forget about "THE" dress—no one will notice the details unless you make a big deal about it. Celebrate what's important!

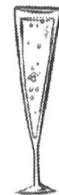

THE LITTLE (BIG) THINGS: CEREMONY & RECEPTION VENUE

We chose to have our wedding reception at a restaurant. The original quote was $130 per person after tax and tip, which was on the high side for us, so we told the event coordinator to help us lower the price. After two weeks of consistent phone calls, the event coordinator finally faxed me a new quote—$100 per person before tax and tip. Being a numbers oriented person, I know the difference between before tax and tip and after tax and tip. It still came out to $129 per person! A $1 difference! I immediately called the coordinator, but did not hear back for ten days.

When we finally spoke, I was perplexed and frustrated, and explained my dismay at the new quote. She said, "Well, you guys do have a lot of food on that menu." Was she serious? I said, "We need to try to bring the price down." She said, "Okay, but can we talk about this tomorrow? I've got three groups coming in five minutes." I reluctantly agreed. And, I never heard from her again. All of this drama three months before our planned wedding date!

—Holly

How To Make It About You

If you haven't signed contracts with the vendor, you should simply walk away, even if there's only three months to the wedding. Don't waste your time with individuals who continue to jerk you around. You are the customer, and you are paying them for a service. Thus, you deserve respect and support for such a big occasion. Countless other vendors will happily offer these things. In the long run, it's probably best that this vendor didn't work out! There may have been a ton of "surprises" waiting for you on the big day!

A friend and her husband were getting married in the family church. They selected the song "We've Only Just Begun" by The Carpenters to be played at the close of the ceremony. The church organist met this request with, "Don't you think it's a bit late for that?" You see, my friend was four months pregnant, and was just starting to show. The self-righteous organist refused to play the song and suggested a few others that she believed were more "appropriate" to their situation.

—Dick

How To Make It About You

When did "begun" begin? None of the rude organist's darn business! If the couple really wants the song played during the ceremony, they should contact the priest. Or simply go to another church that agrees to play the song, even if it isn't the family church. Ultimately, it's up to you whether to subject yourselves to such judgmental individuals.

My husband and I planned our wedding for two years. From the start, we knew the place where we first met was absolutely perfect for the wedding reception. This quaint family restaurant had been operating for over 30 years, and we knew both the reputation of the place and the family. As soon as we got engaged, we called to reserve the date. Six months prior to the wedding, we met to discuss the menu with the new owner, who took over the restaurant when his father passed away one year earlier. Everything was set, so it was one less thing we had to worry about as the day approached. Or so we thought!

A few months prior to the wedding, my husband and I planned to have dinner at the restaurant—but it was closed. We assumed it was only for the evening, and we didn't think about it again until one of our friends called after the wedding invites went out. They wanted to confirm the location of the reception because they'd heard that the restaurant closed down. My husband and I thought our friends were pulling our leg, until they reported that the story was recently in the paper. It seemed the son who took over the business spent the profits gambling and went bankrupt. Two months prior to our wedding, we had to find another venue. But at that point, everything was booked! My husband and I finally found a place out of town and had to contact all the guests with the new location.

—Jane

How To Make It About You

What are the odds that even though you were so prepared, this would happen? Some things you just cannot control. The positive part of this story is that you found out about the restaurant prior to your wedding day. Can you imagine showing up at your reception location only to discover it no longer exists? Task friends and family with contacting all guests regarding the new location. If you are honest with them about the reason for the change, the guests will understand. Also, arrange for a trusted individual to remain at the old location on the wedding day for the first hour of reception, in case any guests have not been informed of the switch.

GO! THE BIG DAY

THE JEWEL OF THE AISLE: HAIR & MAKEUP

One of my bridesmaids loved to apply makeup as though she was starring in a disco movie, if you know what I mean. Yet ironically, she was the only brides-maid who did not want her makeup done before the wedding, even though I offered to pay. On the day, I decided to have all the girls together while we were getting ready for the ceremony. This included putting last minute makeup touches on. The bridesmaid with the disco look arrived last with her makeup complete, and I'm serious when I say she looked like a clown! I'd pre-viously expressed my concerns about this issue to my maid-of-honor, and when we saw how overdone this bridesmaid was, we both just about lost it. My maid-of-honor gave me a look that said, "I'll handle it." To this day, I'm not sure what my maid-of-honor said to her, but by the time the ceremony started, the clown eyes had been removed and the bridesmaid had actually allowed someone to apply tamer eye shadow.

—Lynn

How To Make It About You

Sit down with your bridesmaids before the wedding and communicate your expectations about their appearance on the wedding day. If you want them to look natural, just say so. You have enough to worry about—your bridesmaid's appearance should be last on your list!

I was yet again a bridesmaid in another summer wedding. My family and old pals gathered to celebrate a school friend's union. The theme of the evening quickly became "what aren't we drinking?" We all had a great time at the rehearsal dinner and went to bed at around four in the morning. I woke up three hours later full of sweat with the urge to vomit. I had to meet the bridal

party at the hairdresser by 9 a.m. and at that point, with my head hung over the toilet bowl, I knew I wouldn't make it. Not only had I spent the last half-an-hour vomiting (and vomiting and vomiting), my head was pounding, I had the shakes, and my feet were too swollen to fit into the required brides-maids' shoes. The thought of having to walk down the aisle at one o'clock was frightening! Oh, and my entire pale body was covered with orange streaks. Apparently, after the rehearsal dinner I cooked up the brilliant idea to apply tanning cream—right before I passed out. Honestly, I couldn't have looked pretty if I tried!

To this day it still pains me to recall the cab journey there, but somehow I made it to the hairdresser. In a truly torturous procedure, the evil stylist used over 50 bobby pins to set (stab!) my long hair in the style the bride requested. When the rest of the bridal party went home to get dressed, I made some lame excuse to meet them there, and dashed into another hairdresser down the street. As it was a Saturday morning, I had to beg for an emergency appoint-ment. When the stylist came over to me, I simply cried, "Take them out!" Not only did I arrive late to the bride's house, my hair looked different from all the other bridesmaids, my shoes still didn't quite fit, and my makeup had already faded from sweat, all of which upset the bride.

—Bethany

How To Make It About You

What a lovely picture! All the bride can do in this situation is let it go. Plus, revel big-time in the fact that the endless champagne toasts throughout the reception may offer some sort of payback for her pal's pre-wedding escapades!

One of my bridesmaids was coming in from the South, and I knew that she really liked to do her hair big—yet, I didn't want her big hair to monopolize the wedding pictures. So, I intentionally made hair appointments for all my

bridesmaids at a well-known beauty salon. While I was getting my hair done, my maid-of-honor overheard Ms. South telling her hairdresser that she didn't want her hair pulled back. The maid-of-honor informed her hairdresser of my request. He stepped away to have a word with Ms. South's hairdresser, but she still refused. It took the hairdresser twice as long to style her big, heavy hair into a somewhat tame look. This made Ms. South late for her makeup appointment, and gave everyone else in the bridal party, including me, less than twenty minutes to get dressed once we arrived at the ceremony.

—Nicole

How To Make It About You

A few weeks before the wedding, have a conversation with the bridesmaids about how you prefer their attire and hairstyle to look. If someone like Ms. South starts to fuss on the day, get all the bridesmaids and hairdressers together at the salon and agree that their hair will be worn back. That way, a whole group of people will be on hand to make her look high maintenance. She'll likely cave under peer pressure! Also, if Ms. South's hair appointment is making the group late, give her a deadline. Explain to Ms. South that if her hair is not pulled back by a certain time, she'll have to cancel her makeup appointment. That threat will probably get her moving!

The Jewel of the Aisle: Wedding Dress & Essentials

My bridesmaids surprised me with a bottle of wine for a good luck toast an hour before the ceremony. Thank goodness it was white wine! I was full of nerves and I didn't want to tempt fate! One of the girls preferred red wine to white, so she helped herself to the mini-bar. I didn't like the idea at all, but she had the glass poured before I could even say a word. A too-hard toast and red wine went all over my white dress. All the club soda in the world would not get the red out. I had to ask the photographer not to take too many pictures of the lower part of my dress, since that's where most of it landed.

—Marie

How To Make It About You

Why didn't this bridesmaid just go with the flow, literally, and have one small glass of white wine for the toast? Obviously, she was more concerned about her wine palette than any potential red wine disasters. When the bridesmaid went for the red, you should've clarified that there is no way you'll toast with anything other than white wine or champagne. The bridesmaids with white wine will likely join you for a toast, leaving the bridesmaid with red wine to change wine flavors, or toast by herself. Wear the dress for the ceremony as planned, and if you've forgotten about the stains, for the reception, as well. If the stains are still on your mind, change into a party outfit—yours or one a bridesmaid can lend. And after the wedding, send the selfish bridesmaid your dry cleaning bill!

As the bride, tradition calls for something old, something blue, something borrowed, and something new to wear on your wedding day. I was given my grandmother's pearl earrings to wear, a blue garter, and a new pearl charm bracelet from my mom. These items were packed together with my undergar-

ments. My maid-of-honor was responsible for making sure the items made it to the church the morning of our wedding. But, when I asked her where the items were on the day, she looked at me like a deer caught in headlights. She had accidentally left them in her car the night before, and had driven to the church in her husband's car. I was close to tears because not only were those "something's" missing, but so were the undergarments that helped my dress fit perfectly, too. I was forced to "go on" without all these things. Luckily, the maid-of-honor lent me her mother's earrings to wear and one of the other girls gave me a new bracelet. As for blue, my mom found some blue thread, which I tied around the give-away garter I wore instead. Yes, I had the required items, but it just wasn't the same.

—Missi

How To Make It About You

If possible, have a trusted guest make a quick trip back to the bridesmaid's car to retrieve the items. If this isn't possible, wing it and do not let this issue bother you or your maid-of-honor any further. Although the details seem important at the time, they'll be water under the bridge later in life.

Some people claim that having a little birdie fly by and poop on you is a symbol of good luck. But on your expensive wedding dress while you are posing for official photographs? To heck with luck! To heck with bird s*%t, and to heck with the rest of the bridal party who couldn't stop laughing—and didn't even try to help me get the stuff off my dress. All I wanted to do was scream!

—Katherine

How To Make It About You

In this case, the situation really was about you, but not the "about you" you wanted! Understand that some people laugh because something's funny, and some people laugh out of nervousness. A unique and unexpected situation occurred, and your bridal party laughed for both reasons. Communicate exactly how you need the bridal party's help. Then assign someone to fetch club soda, a towel and a hairdryer if no one has already volunteered. And, before you hit the reception, make a quick stop at 7-11 to play the lotto!

RETURN TO VENDOR!:
FLOWERS

I love daisies and my husband thought they would be a nice touch for our informal wedding ceremony, which was held at my grandparent's small town church. The choice of florists was limited—one shop! The florists seemed nice enough when we ordered the flowers over the phone. Besides, how can you screw up daisies? I arrived in an antique car and as I entered the small church to join my husband-to-be, a hallway full of red greeted me. Red roses everywhere—even my own bouquet! I really had no choice but to accept the wrong flowers. The red rose bouquets and arrangements were very formal, probably my least favorite flower, and completely unlike my daisy-self. When I complained to the florist later on, the owner said they'd lost our order and just assumed red roses would be fine since everyone loves them. Not me!

—Bev

How To Make It About You

If the florist really lost the order, how did they remember the wedding day and location? Hmmm. Sounds like they clearly forgot to order daisies and were forced to make a last minute substitution! On the day, make the florist aware of your dissatisfaction and proceed with the event, as there is nothing you can do. If you don't make an issue about the flowers, no one will notice. Fortunately, many people do like red roses, and you will surely get tons of compliments. Also, after the wedding refuse to pay the florist bill. They messed up—simple as that.

When planning a wedding, normally you provide the florist with flower selections up front. From there, you can only pray the florist brings the right flowers and everything looks perfect. On our wedding day, the flowers were indeed the variety we ordered, but instead of bursting with color, they looked dead.

The flowers must have been at least three days old! When my mother told me about the situation, I was close to tears. After catching my breath, I took a look for myself. I cried when I saw my ruined bouquet. My mom suggested we pull out the flowers that were not fresh, and adorn it with ribbon. It looked fine, but not at all what I had dreamed of. My mom and I chose not to display any flowers inside the hall because there were so few "good" ones.

—Kerry

How To Make It About You

What would Martha do? Informed with an idea of the type of flowers you want, have a few guests with good taste make a quick trip to the local florist or even the supermarket to pick up new flowers. When they return, have them set up a portion of the new flowers and use the reminder for the bridal party's bouquets and boutonnières. Also, make sure your photographer takes a picture of the dead flowers for proof, so you won't have to pay for the ruined bunches. Worry about the unexpected costs after the wedding.

My husband and I had four nieces to select from for our flower girl. I decided that the middle girl would be the best fit. Young enough to be really cute and old enough to handle the responsibility. Of course when I told my mom, she insisted that our flower girl should be the youngest niece, who was three years old. In the end, to avoid conflict, I went with her choice.

On the day of our wedding I was getting dressed at my parents' home when the flower girl's mom called from the hair salon. She wanted to know how I was wearing my hair so my niece's could look similar. I instructed her to pull it back with the sage color ribbon I'd bought, which matched the bridesmaids' dresses. But when the flower girl arrived at the church, she arrived with tons of mismatching flowers weaved crazily throughout her hair—and without the ribbon I'd bought her. Not only that, the girl's mom had altered the dress slightly by removing the ribbon that matched the bridesmaids' dresses, replacing it with a bright pink belt. I was not at all happy, and made sure her mother knew this. One more annoyance.

Just before the ceremony, my littlest niece started crying and refused to go down the aisle. I guess the good thing about this seemingly bad situation was that none of the guests had to see her wild hair and unsightly outfit during the ceremony—although my husband and I did miss out on the flower petals we spent a fortune on.

—Molly

How To Make It About You

Sometimes we try to avoid conflict by not being firm, but in doing so, we only postpone the drama. From the get-go, stand your ground with your mom about the choice of flower girl, and with your niece's mom about her dress and hair. In this case, you might have avoided this mini-tragedy. Just let the frustrating feelings go, and enjoy the day!

On the morning of the wedding, our flowers were to be delivered to the hotel where the bridal party was staying. About an hour before the ceremony, the concierge rang the room to let us know the florist had dropped them off. Right on time! Except they were the wrong flowers. We were also two bouquets short for the bridesmaids and three boutonnières short for the guys. In addition, the mothers were left without anything to carry.

—Janelle

<u>How To Make It About You</u>

What's done is done. At this point, you have three choices: use what you have, find replacements or do without. As with many wedding dilemmas, nobody really knows what should have been but you! Sometimes, not even your husband! If you make the flowers a hugely important issue on the day, you will only make yourself less important. Choose to make your wedding about you!

RETURN TO VENDOR!:
THE PHOTOGRAPHER

Like many couples, we hired a professional photographer, in addition to providing disposable cameras on each table during the reception. When my husband and I came back from our honeymoon, a message was waiting for us on our machine from the "professional" photographer. He informed us that he had somehow managed to damage all of our wedding film. Not a single official wedding picture! Prior to our wedding day, I made sure someone was responsible for the disposable cameras, so at least we had those pictures! However, we later discovered that the appointed person had gotten drunk and failed to collect the cameras at the end of the night. So, the only pictures we had to fill our wedding album were a few candid shots from outside the church, which guests gave us copies of.

—Courtney

How To Make It About You

Ever heard of a "Déjà Vu Wedding Party"? Recreate the wedding by dressing up and inviting all the original guests, and then some! And oblige the photographer to pay for a new photo shoot since he lost the film.

When interviewing the owner of the photography studio who would later capture our wedding photos, we asked questions about price and type of album. However, we failed to ask who the photographer would be, assuming it would be the owner. So you can imagine our surprise when another guy showed up on the wedding day to take our photos. I had wanted to meet him face-to-face and let him get a feel for our personalities. I panicked, but there was nothing we could do. The photographer ended up taking some great portraits of each member of the wedding party, as he was accustomed to portrait photography.

However, he did not take the group pictures we requested (i.e. bride and maid-of-honor, parents).

That was not the end of this photography nightmare! We selected the wedding pictures we wanted from the proofs to be in the "big" wedding book. When we finally looked at it over two months after the wedding, the first picture was of a bride and groom—just not us! We thought the owner grabbed the wrong book, but as he showed us a few other pictures we realized it was indeed not our wedding. After waiting another two months, we finally got our correct book back. It did contain some of our pictures, but not all the ones we had chosen, as the studio had lost several rolls. We were left with a book of proofs!

—Sheri

How To Make It About You

Be as prepared as possible by presenting the photographer with a list of desired group photos on the day, even if you have gone over the requirements in advance. Look at it this way, maybe you went through a bit of stress, but at least you have a picture album with some wedding memories—rather than nothing at all!

A family friend recommended our videographer, and on the wedding day, he seemed very easy going and on top of things. So, when my husband and I returned from our honeymoon, we tried to get in touch with him to view the tape. A month went by, and nothing. We even asked the family friend to track him down. Finally, when we'd given up all hope, we heard from the guy, who then admitted he'd lost the tape. However, our family friend had a different story altogether. Apparently, our wedding was the videographer's first and only job, and he had recorded the entire ceremony on the wrong tape format. The family friend had recommended the guy as a favor because he was just

starting his videography business. We're fortunate this guy wasn't in charge of our photographs, as well!

—Julia

How To Make It About You

Did you preview examples of the videographer's work? Because there weren't any, you would have immediately known the truth about his skills, and might've avoided the disaster completely. Take his tape anyway, demand your money back, and oblige your family friend to watch the tape with you, so he can see how upset you are—and understand why he should never recommend the videographer again. Hey, sometimes the fuzzy memories are better than nothing!

Our photographer came highly recommended from a co-worker. She showed me her own wedding photos, and I agreed that the prints were absolutely beautiful. I also checked out the photographer's portfolio, just to be certain, and it seemed like a great match. Although we paid tons for her services, my husband and I, both artists, agreed that our wedding photographs were a once-in-a-lifetime investment. But, when we got our photographs back, we liked only a handful of them. Overall, the photographs were what I would describe as "funky" or "edgy," which didn't match the tone of our traditional wedding. Plus, most of the group shots we requested were missing. I didn't even have a picture with my parents! But there was nothing my husband and I could do—the wedding day was over.

When the photographer called to see how we liked the photos, I couldn't bring myself to say anything negative. She was a friend of my co-worker! Two fellow artists would appreciate her artistic direction, she remarked. The photographer explained that for once she didn't have to take the boring, posed shots of the wedding party with their mannequin smiles, which made ours such an enjoyable job! Well, glad we could be of service!

—Susan

How To Make It About You

Experimental photography? Not on your dime and not on your wedding day! If you, your families, and the wedding party were prepared to dress up again, the photographer could take some "boring" shots—free of charge, of course—for the photo albums. Who knows? It might be really fun!

My husband and I hired a photographer that was listed on the reception hall's recommendation list. We signed a contract and paid our deposit six months before the wedding day. And three weeks prior, we all got together to go over the list of pictures we wanted. So, you can imagine our surprise when the photographer never showed up to our wedding! We tried reaching the photographer on his cell, and a message said he was out of town on vacation, and would be back two days after our wedding. We ended up relying on family and friends to capture our one and only wedding day.

—Rachel

How To Make It About You

Unbelievable! If you truly want to make your wedding about you, cherish the pictures taken with love by your friends and family. Then, forget the rest! Of course, you can never go back in time, but you'll always have the memories. In addition, get the deposit back and be sure to let the reception hall know what happened so they will take the photographer off their recommended list.

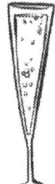

RETURN TO VENDOR!: MUSIC

When my husband and I met the DJ to go over the songs and the order of reception, he told us there would be an assistant with him at no extra charge. After the ceremony, when the DJ introduced us as Mr. & Mrs. S., the first thing I noticed was his assistant. She wore a little number that would lead anyone to believe she was hoping to get picked up. Keep in mind that our reception was at 2:30 p.m., not 2:30 a.m. Her outfit took me by surprise, but then I figured not everyone has good taste, and I was not going to let this issue get me down on my wedding day. As the reception continued and more people started dancing, the DJ's assistant began hitting on all the single guys and a few of the married guys. I'm actually surprised she didn't approach my new husband! Luckily, one of the single guys took the bait.

—Jill

How To Make It About You

The assistant might have thought entertaining the single guys would help make your wedding even more fun, but it sounds like she went overboard! When you initially sign contracts with the DJ, have him put the assistant role in writing and clarify her responsibilities. In addition, specify that she should only wear attire appropriate for your occasion. If she's too much on the day, find a willing volunteer to get the assistant the heck out of the reception. If this isn't a single guy looking to get lucky, find an older, intimidating guy, preferably a father, who doesn't mind escorting her to a car or calling a taxi.

The DJ couldn't find a ride to our wedding, so he called the reception venue to speak to my wife. There was no time to find a replacement, so my wife and

I arranged for an understanding relative to pick up the DJ. Does this boy not know what Yellow Cab is? He was almost two hours late.

—Greg

How To Make It About You

Let's see—how many weddings had the DJ played at and how does he normally get there? These critical questions should be asked before hiring this guy for your special day. Inform the guests that the DJ will be late, so they understand the situation. Also, ask your guests if they have a CD player to use in the meantime. It's a question of mind over matter. If you act like you don't mind the DJ's tardiness, it won't matter to your guests!

My parents insisted on selecting the band. My husband and I reluctantly agreed to it, even though we were so scared that our guests would be treated to music that hadn't been heard since the 50's! Three months before the wedding, my dad found out that the band broke up, but decided not to tell us because he was afraid it would stress us out. Instead, he hired a DJ. My husband and I were shocked to discover the switch when we walked into the wedding reception but we tried to keep calm. The DJ was truly awful. Of course, I probably noticed it more than anyone because he managed to play all of the songs I had asked the original band NOT to play.

—Renee

How To Make It About You

Let's do the twist and spin this situation into a positive one! Simply enjoy yourselves and be happy that you had music. Or you can agree that sometimes no music is better than bad music, and ask the DJ to go home. Or, you could have a trusted individual ask the guests for CDs, even if they have to run to their cars to retrieve them. Then, get the DJ to put his crap to the side and play from the guests' collection. Better yet, ask for volunteers to DJ! Tell the hired DJ to take a back seat and turn the guest-DJ into a fun event! The crowd may really get into it!

RETURN TO VENDOR!:
RECEPTION VENUE

We got married at the same hotel hosting our reception, figuring we would save our out-of-town guests from renting a car. The night before the wedding was very hectic because all my family members were arriving. Additionally, heavy traffic resulted in a late rehearsal start—leaving no time to check in at the hotel and store my luggage. After the rehearsal, the bridesmaids helped me carry my luggage to the room.

The morning of my wedding, it was time to put my tiara on. But…no one knew where it was! My bridesmaids initially kept this from me because they hoped it was just in someone's room or car. After searching for an hour, they finally told me that the tiara was missing and that they had already contacted hotel security for help. Eventually, the bag with the tiara was found in the rehearsal room. Sadly, whoever stole it knew very well that I needed the tiara that day, since the tag on the bag had my name and my wedding date right on the top. I had instantly fallen in love with this tiara. At $500, it was more than the cost of my wedding dress, but I HAD to have it! Thankfully, my bridesmaids, decked out in the bridesmaids' dresses, ran to a local bridal store and purchased a similar tiara.

But wait…the story is not over yet! Since the tiara was valued at over $300, the theft was now considered an act of felony, and as a result, the ceremony site was now a crime scene. Therefore, the hotel was forced to call the police, who taped off the site to investigate and write up a report. Consequently, the ceremony started an hour-and-a-half later than scheduled—a lifetime considering the wedding day's strict schedule! Somewhere out there, someone is wearing my beautiful tiara, and I just pray they needed it more than I did.

—Melanie

How To Make It About You

Hey, if you can't get your friends and family to make your wedding about you, a thief is certainly not going to care! Look at the situation this way—on that day, you lost a tiara, but gained a husband for life. Also, understand that your friends and family came to the wedding for you, not a tiara. They won't care one iota if you don't wear the real one!

My reception hall pulled the ultimate scam. Although we paid for expensive, high-end liquor to be offered to guests, they served cheap liquor during cocktail hour, and well into dinner. My husband and I didn't realize the con until my father requested a name brand drink and was told by a waiter that it wasn't being served. My husband and I went ballistic! But when we were told the manager who arranged the contract wasn't even there, we realized we'd have to deal with the issue after our honeymoon.

—Karen

How To Make It About You

Did you think you were the only ones this happened to? Nope. The old switcharoo trick happens all the time! After you come back from the honeymoon, demand not only the difference between the cheap and expensive liquor costs, but also a full refund. The reception staff was clearly trying to con you out of money when you were most vulnerable.

Our friends held their wedding reception in the ballroom of a country club. On the day of the wedding, the guests were initially guided to a small room in the club for cocktails. After about an hour, we started to wonder why the real reception hadn't already begun, since we hadn't been served appetizers, and

everyone was starving. Thirty minutes later, the guests were finally escorted to another room—but again, it wasn't the ballroom. There were 120 people crammed into a teeny room appropriate for 60—and with no dance floor. Our table sat 12 people, so let's just say it wasn't easy to eat when the food finally arrived an hour later—almost thee hours after the church ceremony. The guests started to make jokes about the bride and groom trying to skimp on the costs, until the bride's father got up to apologize. He explained that the bride and groom had indeed reserved the ballroom, but a prior wedding had started late and did not finish as early as expected. Around 8 p.m., the guests were at long last allowed to enter the ballroom. The band started playing and a dance floor, host-bar, and the cake were all waiting to be enjoyed.

—Roger

How To Make It About You

This is your wedding day, not an assembly line! The reception venue is at fault for booking two weddings back to back. If the venue only has one big room, make sure that the agreement states the exact times your party has the venue reserved. If the venue doesn't meet the times on your day, you should automatically get a percentage of the money back, no questions asked—plus a free evening in the ballroom for another celebration. If possible, make an exclusive booking for your reception venue. Although it might cost a bit more, this will save future headaches—and rule out situations like this before they occur.

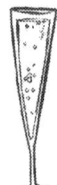

YOUR (THEIR) TIME TO SHINE: THE CEREMONY

When I was a young girl, I watched wide-eyed as Diana became a princess in front of the entire world. Hers was the kind of elaborate, fairy tale wedding I dreamed of for myself. So when my husband and I were married on a lovely June day in the church we both grew up attending, I tried my best to recreate the princess setting. Five-foot pillar candles lined the long regal maroon carpet aisle and hundreds of beautiful flowers adorned the front of the church. My dress was a Princess Diana look-alike, complete with a veil that flowed eight feet behind me. As I walked down the aisle with my father, I truly felt like a princess on her way to meet Prince Charming.

As I reached my husband at the altar, I gave my father a kiss and then leaned down to give one to my mother. When I did, my eight-foot veil passed right over one of the pillar candles and ignited. To make a long story short, my mother screamed, my father ripped the veil off my head and threw it onto the ground, the carpet caught on fire, my matron-of-honor fainted, and everyone evacuated the church. Luckily, the fire was put out and no one got hurt. But sadly, my veil and dress were ruined, my hair and makeup had to be completely redone and my husband and I had to be married hours later at the reception. We laugh about it now, but at the time it was completely devastating!

—Elizabeth

How To Make It About You

What a royal catastrophe! Not having pillar candles may have prevented this mishap, but you should always aim to have the wedding of your dreams. Look, things happen that you cannot control. So your dress was ruined, the wedding was late and you had to get married at the reception hall. But at least no one got hurt, and you walked away certain that none of the guests would ever forget your wedding! What seems so important and serious at the time may be forgotten and even humorous in the long run. Count your blessings!

As my father walked me down the aisle, he turned to me and said, "It's not too late to back out." I'm sure he thought his words would comfort me, but his voice echoed throughout the hall. All of our guests heard him—including my new husband!

—Jasmine

How To Make It About You

Well, you probably did want to back out after he made the surprise statement—from total embarrassment! Your father might have thought his comment would relax you, but he actually created a scene that no bride wishes for on her wedding day. Explain to your husband that your father was only trying to say something reassuring. You could also ask your father to make a joke about his inappropriate comment during the speeches, but then you always run the risk of it backfiring!

My husband and I were married in a conservative church ceremony. For the blessing, the priest instructed us to kneel before the altar. Unknown to us, one of the ushers taped "HELP ME!" to the bottom of my husband's shoes for a joke. So when he knelt down, the congregation burst into laughter. The serious priest, and both my husband and I didn't know how to react. Had somebody passed wind? Maybe my dress had ridden up in the back! Not until the

reception did we discover the truth. This is my lasting memory of our wedding ceremony.

—Nancy

How To Make It About You

You may have heard a similar story before and maybe even laughed about it. But when it happened to you on your wedding day, the joke didn't seem so funny, did it? There is a time and a place for jokes at a wedding—preferably at reception speeches. The usher was only trying to draw attention to himself as the jester. Just let this insensitive behavior go. To do otherwise would just add fuel to the usher's fire.

You can't have a wedding without the rings, right? Well, that nearly happened to me. Or, so I thought! My husband's family is full of practical jokers, mainly his brothers and uncles. On our wedding day, when the minister asked for the rings, they had conspired with my husband's best man to act as if he'd forgotten them. Seemingly flustered, he asked my husband's brother if he'd happened to pick them up. His brother patted his pockets, shook his head and asked his father. His father asked his uncle, who asked his son, who asked his brother. This carried on all the way down the front rows, much to the amusement of the congregation. My husband and I were stressing out! We thought the ceremony would be delayed until the best man, with a sly grin on his face, exclaimed, "Here they are!" I swear I could have strangled each and every one of them!

—Stephanie

How To Make It About You

As you are well aware, a wedding is not the time to panic the bride or groom. A badly timed or badly executed practical joke can ruin everyone's memories of the wedding ceremony—especially the bride and groom's. Your husband should have had a serious conversation with the known jokers in his family and asked them to abstain from self-seeking behavior by promising they will not make a scene during the ceremony. If you choose to, give guests an outlet for gags at the reception. During speeches, on the dance floor, or at the bar would have been a more appropriate time.

YOUR (THEIR) TIME TO SHINE: SPEECHES

At the end of his speech, my husband's best man instructed our 200 guests to turn over their placemats, and join him in a toast to the end of my husband's single life and the beginning of his married life. As everyone began to do so, the room fell completely silent. On the bottom of each placemat, the best man had taped two pictures with accompanying text. On the left side was a picture of my husband at his bachelor party a week beforehand, drunk and with a naked stripper on his lap. The text below read, "Goodbye, balls." On the right side was possibly the worst picture of me ever taken. No makeup, a huge pimple on my chin, messy hair, flabby stomach, and stuffing my face with pizza. The text below read, "Hello, ball and chain!" No one was even remotely amused—the least of all my parents, who stormed out angrily. My dad wanted to kill the guy AND my husband. I was just utterly embarrassed.

—Michelle

How To Make It About You

Yikes! This is bad. Very bad. What a jerk—and that's putting it mildly! The best man's behavior is completely inexcusable, and you and your family have every right to be upset. If the best man has consistently played the clown, he will likely fall into that role on the wedding day. Obviously, he thought it was more important for his joke to go off well and chose not to consider that it might offend you and—um—the entire reception. Before the wedding, have your husband clarify that this guy won't be doing or saying anything inappropriate. Following the fiasco, have your husband demand that he apologize not only to you and your family, but also to the guests. Then ask him to throw away all the placemats, take a hike, and let you get on with your wedding reception.

My wife and I gave short-notice invitations to our parents, siblings, and their immediate families when we eloped. Perched atop a mountain range over-looking the coast, the day was perfectly unforgettable—full of energy and love. By dinner, my amazingly charming and successful father-in-law was amaz-ingly drunk, and insisted that he make a toast. His words of wisdom? "To our wives and our mistresses, may they never meet." A perfectly unforgettable day!

—Colin

How To Make It About You

Weddings and alcohol often bring out the unexpected in people, especially fathers-of-the-bride or groom. Accept the joke for what it was, and enjoy what sounds like a beautiful day. Remember, it's a good story to tell in the future!

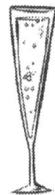

During our reception, the best man made a beautiful speech, my matron-of-honor read a poem, and then my parents said a few words. Next, an usher got up to say something. When we thought the speeches were over, a friend of mine grabbed the microphone. The only planned speeches were the best man's and matron-of-honor's. The additional speeches were no big deal, except that my friend who got up was not prepared, so she began walking the guests through every detail of our friendship, which began at age six. In addition, the speech made absolutely no sense, even to me! After about fifteen minutes, I think she realized she should stop because most of the guests got up to grab a drink from the bar.

—Erin

How To Make It About You

Wedding guests do want to contribute on such an emotional day. However, it is not appropriate for anyone to make a banquet speech. Discuss the specific order of speeches with the DJ or Band Leader in advance, and ask them to quickly check with you before anyone else grabs the microphone. If you hire a videographer, it might also make sense for them to announce that every guest will have the opportunity to say a few words throughout the evening, as the camcorder makes its way around the tables.

EAT, DRINK AND BE MARRIED: THE CAKE

One of the few things I splurged on was a beautiful, one-of-a-kind, five-tier wedding cake with fondant frosting and fresh flowers. The wedding reception staff told me that the $400 cake was lovely, but unfortunately my husband and I never saw it because—it fell over! Turns out that the cake designer didn't secure the base well enough. My videographer was able to capture the pre-demolished cake, but, needless to say, I was very, very upset. Basically, it looked more like a flower centerpiece than a cake, even after the sympathetic reception staff tried to put it back together. Just when I came to the realization that we couldn't repair the cake, that we would miss out on a traditional cake cutting ceremony, and worst of all, that our guests would be deprived of dessert, my wedding coordinator offered a piece of advice that only set me off again—she told me to get over it!

—Teddi

How To Make It About You

Your beloved cake! Look, you can't control what comes out of the insensitive wedding coordinator's big mouth, but you can control how you react to her nasty comment. Brush it off, see the humor in the situation and have the coordinator arrange for the bakery to rush over a new cake—or two—pronto.

My mom and I shopped all over for the perfect wedding cake, and finally came across a lady with great prices and high quality cakes. In the first meeting, we explained that we wanted a basket-weave cake decorated with fresh flowers. In the second meeting, we let her know that our family florist would select and arrange the flowers on the cake. Immediately, she became defensive and said that while it was okay for our florist to select the flowers, she was the

one who would arrange them on the cake. We stressed that we would prefer to have our florist arrange the flowers since we were comfortable with his artistic style. Yet, the cake lady continued to insist that she arrange the flowers, since the cake was her creation and that the arrangement of the flowers were included in that creation. Last time I checked, I was the one buying the cake! To make a long story short, on our wedding day the cake lady initially arranged the flowers on the cake. As soon as she left the premises, I made sure our florist rearranged them. In the end, and even though it was a stressful process, the cake turned out beautifully!

—Christin

How To Make It About You

What a crazy control freak—the cake lady, that is. Simply use another bakery that will give you exactly what you want, no questions asked. It's your money, and you get to call the shots! Don't you have better things to do on your wedding day than rearrange flowers?

It took four visits with my husband to various bakeries to select the flavor of our wedding cake. We decided on lemon, given that my husband was allergic to chocolate. My mother and I shopped styles at different bakeries until we found the perfect one. At our reception, while cutting our cake, I looked at my mom in shock—the inside of the cake was chocolate flavored! And my husband can't have anything with even the slightest chocolate flavor. He cringed when he realized the mistake. I whispered, "I swear it was supposed to be lemon. Ask my mom!" My husband fed me the cake anyway because the DJ started the chant. When it was my turn, I only gave him frosting.

—Rebecca

<u>How To Make It About You</u>

Smile, laugh it off, and make light of the situation! Guests will probably get a kick out of the irony in it all! The cake cutting is only five minutes of the entire wedding, anyway. Serve the cake to the guests as planned, and after the honeymoon, refuse to pay the cake bill—you did not receive the service you paid for. In addition, have the bakery deliver a new lemon cake for your one-month anniversary. And, enjoy every last bite!

EAT, DRINK AND BE MARRIED: FOOD & ALCOHOL

Our guests were treated to a full sit-down dinner, complete with surf and turf. Everyone was impressed with the meal until two hours afterward. One minute the dance floor was packed, and then all of the sudden we noticed a few guests holding their stomachs, complaining of pains. The next thing we knew, they were running full force to the restrooms. My husband and I started feeling stomach pains, too. We ended up inside the bathrooms with half the guests for the next few hours. The restaurant later figured out that the shrimp was bad and, needless to say, what we thought was going to be a long night ended abruptly with 70% of the guests sick with food poisoning.

—Marisa

How To Make It About You

First things first. As the bride and groom, insist that you get first priority in the bathrooms! This situation probably couldn't have been avoided, but you might want to stick with "safe" foods for the wedding reception. After your honeymoon, throw a vegetarian-only post-wedding party with all the same guests—at the restaurant's full expense.

We had eighty guests at our wedding and reserved eighty bottles of expensive wine to be served throughout dinner. My husband and I knew that all the bottles probably wouldn't be used, but wanted to have enough, just in case. We arranged to have the reception venue's Master of Ceremony (MC) do a quick bottle count with us after dinner. We would only pay for bottles used. At the end of dinner, my husband and I couldn't locate the MC, so we found the headwaiter and did a bottle count with her. The used bottles came to 58.

We asked her to contact the MC and let him know the total count, and then went on to our reception next door.

When it came time to pay the final bill, the MC charged my husband and I for the full 80 bottles. We explained that we only used 58, and that we had verified this count with the headwaiter. The MC contacted the headwaiter and she insisted that we had used all 80 bottles—an outright lie! Just what we wanted to deal with on our way to the honeymoon! Fortunately, one of the guests overheard the argument. She informed the MC and us that most of the wait staff had joined our reception party after my husband and I had gone to bed, and had helped themselves to the unused bottles of wine! Thank goodness for friends!

—Jean

How To Make It About You

Instead of assuming the headwaiter would pass on the correct message, speak directly to the MC after dinner. Otherwise, like that childhood game of telephone, the intended communication may get distorted along the way. Maybe a member of the bridal party or one of your parents could track him down. In addition, assign someone to oversee important, cost-related issues on the day, so you aren't forced to deal with it during your wedding weekend.

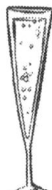

We decided to have a backyard BBQ to cut costs. My boss suggested a butcher for the pre-marinated meat. The shop had supplied the food for our work cookouts for many years, so it seemed easy enough. The day before the wedding, I arrived at the butcher and found they didn't take credit cards. As I turned to leave for the cash machine down the street, I approached the glass meat case. The displayed meat looked old and smelled more than un-fresh. Plus, flies were swarming around and actually sitting on the meat! I was sick to my stomach. Then I noticed a "C" rating on the window, and felt even

more disgusted! Needless to say, I drove around town until I found a quality butcher.

—Ellie

How To Make It About You

Ew. A "C" rating typically means, "C you for not much longer, because we're about to be shut down!" Always be careful with recommendations, especially food recommendations, as people's tastes are so different. Check out the butcher well in advance before making any commitments. The last thing you need are guests complaining about the food or getting sick on the wedding day! And if things go wrong with the meat at the last minute, find someone else who can scramble to find an alternative. A father, uncle, cousin or usher would likely welcome this hunter-gatherer role!

NOT ON THEIR GUEST BEHAVIOR: WEDDING ATTIRE

Our spring wedding was to be held in the South. Humidity would definitely be a factor. So, I told my bridesmaids months before that they did not have to wear pantyhose with their open-toed sandals. The day of the wedding, my sister, who was the matron-of-honor, told me that some of the girls wanted to wear patterned control pantyhose—which they didn't bring up when we discussed the attire four months prior. Waiting for me to find out on the day of my wedding was not the ideal time to share! As it ended up, half of the girls wore the pantyhose, and the other half did not. So, we look mismatched in all the pictures. It wasn't a huge problem, but at the time, it was just one more thing that I had to deal with right before our wedding.

—Cori

How To Make It About You

You often hear stories about brides making their bridesmaids wear something bizarre or hideous. In accepting the role of a bridesmaid, one must be prepared to wear something out of the ordinary. Maybe it's not fair, but in the end, the bride's wedding day is about her, not them. Yes, the bridesmaids can voice their concerns, but if the bride doesn't waver, the bridesmaids should let go of the issue. Moreover, they shouldn't wait for the day of the bride's wedding to tell her they don't want to wear something. Enjoy the day as the bride and not as the fashion police—don't get hot and bothered about little things like pantyhose!

I didn't find out until the day of our wedding that one of my bridesmaids was having difficulty getting into her dress. When we ordered them, she'd just had a baby. To play it safe we got her a dress two sizes larger, even though she was certain there would be plenty of time before my wedding to lose the weight.

Unknown to me, two months before the wedding, she called the dress shop to buy a larger size, but the dress was no longer available. When we were all getting dressed on the day of the wedding, my bridesmaid was actually squeezed into the dress. Yet it was so tight that she put on a white sweater to cover up. It looked okay, but I didn't want her to wear it for the pictures or when she walked down the aisle. She complied for the ceremony, but as soon as it was done, the white sweater went back on, and it didn't come off for the rest of the night. As I anticipated, she looked out of place next to the other bridesmaids in the pictures. Well, what could I have done?

—Maddy

How To Make It About You

In an ideal world, everyone in the bridal party would make a point to focus on you and try hard to make your day as wonderful as possible. Instead of focusing on themselves, the bridal party would think, *"How can I help?"* Does this happen? Rarely! At the end of the day, if having the bridesmaid not wear the sweater for the pictures is so important, than be more assertive. Put your foot down, girl!

One of my bridesmaids dresses in a tacky fashion. I only had two bridesmaids, and when I asked them to help me pick out their dresses, she was not available. I told her to pick whatever dress she liked, as long it came in periwinkle, our wedding color. She selected a dress that was conservative and plain. The morning of my wedding, the two bridesmaids met at my home. The bridesmaid who dressed in bad taste had changed the whole dress! She cut a huge slit in the front above her knee so her thighs would show, she put sequins all over the front, and cut the back, which did not allow her to wear a bra. I couldn't believe my eyes, but remained composed and just said, "You changed it." Apparently, the original dress did not suit her taste, so according to the bridesmaid she, "altered it slightly." Simple and slightly it was not. Trashy

and tacky it was, just like her! Oh, and did I mention she was my new sister-in-law?

—Caroline

How To Make It About You

Jeez, at least she could have shared her concerns with you before the day. Like Popeye said, *"I am what I am what I am!"* The tacky dress is not a reflection of you—only on your new sister-in-law. Ideally, get your two bridesmaids together when the dresses come in, and have a fun pre-wedding fashion show. Then, clarify that the dress is not to be significantly altered without your approval. On the day, if you can't fix the dress, let it go, or hand her a sweater to cover up.

Why is it that some women insist on wearing white to a wedding? I was taught that a female guest should never, ever wear white, as she would naturally compete for attention with the bride on her big day. I guess I assumed that most people followed this unwritten rule, but two women at our wedding were dressed in white from head to toe.

—Tanya

How To Make It About You

Ah, they'll get you every time. Those women, young to old, single, married or divorced, who arrive at your big party thinking *they* are the star-of-the-day. At most weddings, at least one woman will dress entirely in white. Simple common sense would help guests figure out that wearing white is disrespectful to the bride, who will very obviously be wearing white, too! Just laugh it off as showy behavior!

My conservative parents and in-laws were members of the country club where we planned to marry, and they made it clear that the wedding party and guests were to respect the formal dress requirement of the country club. The invitations included instructions for this dress code and our number for any questions. As it happened, a college sorority sister showed up wearing something more appropriate for a wet tee-shirt contest than a formal southern union. Throughout my wedding day, the guests paid more attention to the girl's slutty attire instead of me—the bride! This included my husband, who stood at the bar with his pals, cracking jokes.

—Christina

How To Make It About You

"I do solemnly swear by taking this oath of sisterhood, that I will make all attempts to upstage my other sorority sisters at their weddings. No matter what it takes, I will do my best to ruin their day by working hard to preserve the most important rule, set forth by our founding sisters those many years ago: '*Always remember Me, Me, Me.*' For the love of sisterhood!" Simply put, the way a guest dresses is out of your control, so let the issue go and have fun. After the wedding, reevaluate why your "sister" would behave so inappropriately.

I was a bridesmaid in my girlfriend's wedding party. She had invited a long-time friend of ours, even though we had grown distant from her because of her increasing bad habits. You see, she was known to wear sleazy looking out-

fits, and she could never understand why men would approach her to ask, "How much?" even though she was married! As we arrived five minutes before the ceremony, all of us bridesmaids were discussing what this gal would wear. So, guess who we see walking up the church steps? This was her outfit: a huge red hat, a short red leather skirt, a red see-through sweater with a camisole underneath, red gloves, red pumps, and red panty hose. We all had a huge laugh, although the bride was a bit annoyed. Her "lady in red" (or is it "lady is a tramp's"!) attire also disgusted the best man. During his speech he wanted to embarrass her, but at the last minute changed his mind because he realized doing so would give her more attention than she had already received.

—Kellie

How To Make It About You

Maybe in addition to indicating what type of wedding attire guests should wear on the invitations, we should also include the statement, "NO RED OR WHITE ALLOWED!" Although it's an insult to the bride, you should almost expect this fading friend's self-oriented behavior, and just let it go. It's out of your control. The *"lady in red"* will likely dress as she always does—sleazy

NOT ON THEIR GUEST BEHAVIOR: OUT-OF-CONTROL DRINKING

My cousin was not invited to our wedding, but showed up anyway with his girlfriend in tow. Both got drunk and in full view of everyone at the reception, they stepped out onto the balcony and got high. Even later, and by now even more drunk, he stole money from the bartender's tip jar, got into a fistfight with his girlfriend, and even attempted to drive home, but steered into a ditch and wrecked the car instead. My husband's cousin, a police officer, saw everything, and threatened my badly behaved cousin with arrest. Unfortunately, his girlfriend refused to press charges, but did leave him stranded at the reception, where he was forced to call his mother and cry like a baby for a ride home!

—Meredith

How To Make It About You

Are you sure this isn't an episode of *COPS*? Funny, the tough guys always act like children in the end, don't they? Without fail, some guests, and especially family, will decide to act poorly at happy occasions, especially when alcohol is involved. Have the police officer kick out both uninvited guests, or just let them embarrass themselves! Stealing money from the tip jar? What losers!

I attended a wedding about six years ago where the groom went out for his bachelor party the night before the wedding, and arrived for the 11 a.m. wedding without a wink of sleep. He and his groomsmen decided to continue the drinking up until the moment he stood at the altar. All the guests knew he was

drunk and, luckily, he managed to say his fiancé's name and "I do" during the vows. I think he finally sobered up sometime during the cake cutting.

—Ginnie

How To Make It About You

If your husband can't be bothered to make the wedding about YOU BOTH, then why should anyone else? What a way to start married life! Never, ever have a bachelor or bachelorette party the night before the wedding. If this is unavoidable because of his buddies' schedules, arrange for a trusted individual to make sure that your husband is sober and rested for the ceremony.

Having witnessed my fair share of weddings spoiled by drunken guests, my husband and I wanted to make sure the same situation didn't happen at ours. We instructed the bartender to not serve anyone who was visibly drunk. By the time the cake cutting rolled around, my aunt's second husband was already smashed, so the bartender cut him off. The drunken uncle proceeded to make a huge scene, verbally and physically threatening the bartender, then yelling about what a "terrible wedding" ours was. His exact words were, "This wedding sucks!" As he stormed out of the reception with my aunt following close behind, he screamed that he wished he'd never come in the first place. My thoughts exactly!

—Susan

How To Make It About You

Be happy that your uncle left the reception. Rest assured that he, not you, will be the one who is embarrassed the next day when he doesn't remember anything, or if he manages to recall how stupid he acted! Within minutes, all the guests will forget the drunken uncle and focus on having a good time. Follow suit!

HOW TO MAKE YOUR WEDDING ABOUT YOU

+ Stay true to exactly how you and your partner want to celebrate your love. It's your day, and it's not only okay, but also your right to make it about you!

+ If you truly want to call all the shots, foot the bill.

+ Present a "united front" on every wedding issue. Support one another and each other's wishes. *"This is what WE want"* is a very powerful statement.

+ Lay down the law! Early on in the wedding planning, communicate your expectations, as well as the consequences, if they are not met.

+ Those who support your decisions, even though they may not agree with them, are your true friends. If others try to make your wedding about them, perhaps they are not true friends after all.

+ Beware of conditional offers to help. There's no such thing as "free lunch."

+ Recognize that everyone, including you, brings personal agendas to weddings.

+ Don't expect people to change who they are just because it's your wedding day—relationships and behavioral patterns exist well beforehand.

+ Remember that it's always possible to turn things around—turn negative situations into positive ones!

+ Accept that if people act inappropriately, it's a reflection on them, not on you.

+ Assemble a trusted team of individuals to troubleshoot during the wedding planning and on the day.

+ Keep in mind that a successful wedding is dependent on good planning. Give yourself time, options, and support.

✦ Don't stand for bad service. Other vendors will happily welcome your business.

✦ Sometimes the best solution is to let it go or walk away.

✦ Remember that you and your partner's love is the real reason you are getting married. Although it may not seem like it at the time, everything else is irrelevant.

✦ Lastly, remember you are not alone! As this book shows, every bride has a story or two—or two hundred!

WE COULDN'T HAVE SAID
IT BETTER OURSELVES

While I may not be able to pass on much advice that hasn't already been given, I can say this: Make sure that, at the end of the day, your wedding is about who you are and who your husband-to-be is. Share and include a part of yourselves in every aspect of the planning, from the service to the honeymoon. I often found that it became very easy to make it someone else's wedding. The mother-in-law who wants you to wear that hideous veil, the brother who just can't make it the month you had in mind, the friend who won't eat the food because she's vegan. The list goes on and on.

Make your wedding your own—and no one else's. And when the bridal shower is done, the details of the ceremony are long forgotten, and the honeymoon is over, close that chapter of your life, and don't regret a single thing!

—Audra

So many women during our wedding planning stages expressed to me their girlhood fantasies for a perfect wedding. Every detail had been set long before and replayed in their dreams over the years, altered slightly to accommodate the current boyfriend, a parent's messy break-up or perhaps a change in sexual orientation. I never had those wedding dreams and so felt unfettered by what that moment might be. In truth, I didn't much care about my wedding,

aside from wanting a doorway of ritual to pass through into a beautiful marriage.

With our families back in the U.S. and us living in Asia, my husband and I sat down to discuss our expectations. We knew it would be difficult to handle the details from abroad and heard horror stories about friends who had tried.

The one thing my husband and I agreed on from the onset was that our marriage was about us. We wanted our wedding to be about sharing our love and commitment with our family and friends—bringing them in as participants to the community of love and support that would sustain us in hard times, as well as share with us and magnify our good times. The details would just be icing on the cake! We especially tried to accommodate and honor our parents, and they were major decision-makers in our planning process. At the end of the day, we had two nice weddings—one Chinese and one Western. Both reflected the great importance and the high priority my husband and I placed on family and friends—and most of all, us.

—Diana

Being a caterer, I had every detail of my wedding planned out. Food from our favorite restaurant was ordered. Wine and champagne was stocked. We reserved a tent, tables and chairs, and flowers by the bucket full. We also drew on the many talents of our friends and family. A phenomenal pastry chef designed a unique coconut and lime cake. My DJ friend was booked, my daughter agreed to play a couple of songs on her flute, and my two dear friends would sing during the ceremony. My husband and our kids would carry our rings. The date was set and the invitations sent. And then a few weeks before the wedding, my world turned upside down.

My youngest daughter was diagnosed with diabetes and we spent several sad days in the hospital learning how to cope. I was devastated, heartbroken, exhausted and in shock. I couldn't bring myself to sleep or eat, and lost ten pounds in one week. No problem fitting into that wedding dress! There was so much information to absorb about a disease I knew nothing about, and I had to learn how to be a round-the-clock caregiver. In addition, it was hard to accept that your beloved child is inflicted with a disease that can not only have horrible long-term complications, but can become a medical emergency at any given moment. I have to say this was the worst week of my life.

I insisted that the ceremony and reception planning would continue. But in reality, I was a complete basket case. Finally, on the day before the wedding, I realized that I couldn't bring myself to do it. My husband and I agreed we would still have a ceremony, but with only the judge and a few close friends and family. Ironically, it was the perfect time to get married, "in sickness and in health." No reception, no food, no music, no fanfare—just my husband and I exchanging vows. That's all that mattered to us anyway. We cancelled everything. My friends called the seventy guests and uninvited them. Can you imagine?

Well, on the "big day," I wasn't expecting much, except to be married to my sweetheart. My two daughters and I put on our pretty dresses, and it was so sweet getting ready with them, braiding each others' hair, putting on makeup and jewelry, and flouncing around. At that moment I knew so distinctly what's really important in life—love and family.

When my friends arrived, they brought us all sorts of surprises! One of my closest friends organized a reception for us, asking different friends to each take on a responsibility. The scrumptious coconut lime wedding cake arrived after all, as well as so many other culinary delights. One friend brought vases of flowers, and even designed an impromptu bouquet for me to carry. Candles were lit all over our house, a CD player with music was set up, and our kitchen was transformed into a banquet hall. Our five combined children stood up with us, and my friend sang. My husband said the most beautiful words to me as close friends and parents witnessed our union. It wasn't the wedding we had planned, but everything was perfect.

I guess the moral of my wedding story is that future brides and grooms should remember that even the best-laid plans can go awry. Bear in mind that at the center of the numerous details and tasks lay the real reason you are getting married. So many things just don't matter in the long run—at least not enough to stress out. Enjoy the planning, and let the little "issues" go. Enjoy the ceremony, and enjoy your marriage. However it turns out will be just right!

—Wendy

ABOUT THE AUTHORS

Jean Ramsden

Orchestrating her own international wedding that included guests from 9 months to 90 years who hailed from seven different countries, was right up Jean's alley. Having produced international media for all ages, Jean is well versed in delivering projects on time, within budget and under pressure, as well as in dealing with devilish details and diva-like attitudes. Her first taste of event planning came as Events Chair and President of Kappa Delta, her university sorority. Jean holds a B.S. from Cornell and a Masters from Harvard. She is currently an entertainment consultant and freelance writer, and resides with her husband and daughter in Los Angeles, California.

Corinne Weldon

Before getting married, Corinne was a member of over a dozen wedding parties. When it came time to plan her own wedding (at the ripe "old" age of 37!), she thought it would be a breeze, as she has tons of experience dealing with people's behavior and organizations. As President of the Coral Gables, Florida Junior Chamber, Corinne managed several hundred volunteers and planned charity events. She has worked in human resources for over twenty years where she has admittedly, "seen it all." She holds a B.S. from the University of Phoenix. Corinne resides with her husband and son in Los Angeles, California.

Please visit our website at www.ItsMyWeddingSite.com

978-0-595-36032-1
0-595-36032-7

www.ingramcontent.com/pod-product-compliance
Lightning Source LLC
Chambersburg PA
CBHW051432280526
45785CB00003B/1257